LEVEL

5

Jacob's Ladder

READING COMPREHENSION PROGRAM

Grades 7–9

LEVEL

5

Jacob's Ladder
Reading Comprehension Program

Grades 7–9

Joyce VanTassel-Baska, Ed.D., &
Tamra Stambaugh, Ph.D.

PRUFROCK PRESS INC.
WACO, TEXAS

Prufrock Press Inc.
P.O. Box 8813
Waco, TX 76714-8813
Phone: (800) 998-2208
Fax: (800) 240-0333
http://www.prufrock.com

Contents

Acknowledgments

A special thank you to Ashley Thomas, Assistant Coordinator of Programs for Talented Youth at Vanderbilt University, for her assistance in editing draft copies of the manuscript and writing the biographies.

Part I: Teachers' Guide to Jacob's Ladder Reading Comprehension Program

Introduction to *Jacob's Ladder, Level 5*

Jacob's Ladder, Level 5 is a supplemental reading program that implements targeted readings from short stories, poetry, and nonfiction sources. With this program, students engage in an inquiry process that moves from lower order to higher order thinking skills. Starting with basic literary understanding, students learn to critically analyze texts by determining implications and consequences, generalizations, main ideas, and/or creative synthesis. Suggested for students in grades 7–9 to enhance reading comprehension and critical thinking, *Jacob's Ladder 5* tasks are organized into six skill ladders: A–F. Each ladder focuses on a different skill. Students "climb" each ladder by answering lower level questions before moving to higher level questions or rungs at the top of each ladder. Each ladder stands alone and focuses on a separate critical thinking component in reading.

Ladder A focuses on implications and consequences. By leading students through sequencing and cause and effect activities, they learn to draw implications and consequences from readings. Ladder B focuses on making generalizations. Students first learn to provide details and examples, and then move to classifying and organizing those details in order to make generalizations. Ladder C focuses on themes. Students begin by identifying setting and characters and then make inferences about the literary situation. Ladder D focuses on creative synthesis by leading students through paraphrasing and summarizing activities. Ladder E focuses on readers' emotional responses to the literature by understanding emotion, expressing it, and then channeling it productively. Ladder F provides an emphasis on metacognition by engaging learners in reflecting on the literature read and on their own applications of it for their lives. Table 1 provides a visual representation of the six ladders and corresponding objectives for each ladder and rung.

The *Jacob's Ladder* series consists of five levels: 1, 2, 3, 4, and 5. All five levels contain short stories, poetry, nonfiction selections including biographies, and at least two commensurate ladders for each selection, with the exception of Level 1, in which some reading selections have one ladder. *Jacob's Ladder 1* is recommended for students in grades 2–3, *Jacob's Ladder 2* is recommended for students in grades 4–5, and *Jacob's Ladder 3* is recommended for students in grades 5–6. The newest books in the series, Levels 4 and 5, are recommended for grades 7–9. However, teachers may find that they want to vary usage beyond the recommended levels, depending on student abilities. Evidence suggests that the curriculum can be successfully implemented with gifted learners as well as promising learners and advanced readers at different grade levels.

Ladder A: Focus on Implications and Consequences

The goal of Ladder A is to develop prediction and forecasting skills by encouraging students to make connections among the information provided. Starting with sequencing, students learn to recognize basic types of change that occur within a text. Through identifying cause and effect relationships, students then can judge the impact of certain events. Finally, through recognizing consequences and implications, students predict future events as logical and identify both short- and long-term consequences by judging probable outcomes based on data provided. The rungs are as follows:

- **Ladder A, Rung 1, Sequencing:** The lowest rung on the ladder, sequencing, requires students to organize a set of information in order, based on their reading (e.g., List the steps of a recipe in order).

- **Ladder A, Rung 2, Cause and Effect:** The middle rung, cause and effect, requires students to think about relationships and identify what causes certain effects and/or what effects were brought about because of certain causes (e.g., What causes a cake to rise in the oven? What effect does the addition of egg yolks have on a batter?).

Table 1
Goals and Objectives of *Jacob's Ladder* by Ladder and Rung

	Ladder A	Ladder B	Ladder C	Ladder D	Ladder E	Ladder F
Rung 1	**A1: Sequencing** — Students will be able to list, in order of importance or occurrence in the text, specific events or plot summaries.	**B1: Details** — Students will be able to list specific details or recall facts related to the text or generate a list of ideas about a specific topic or character.	**C1: Literary Elements** — Students will be able to identify and explain specific story elements such as character, setting, or poetic device.	**D1: Paraphrasing** — Students will be able to restate lines read using their own words.	**E1: Understanding Emotion** — Students will be able to explain how emotion and feeling are conveyed in a text and/or their personal experience.	**F1: Planning and Goal Setting** — Students will be able to explain and design an outline or plan given certain stimuli.
Rung 2	**A2: Cause and Effect** — Students will be able to identify and predict relationships between character behavior and story events and their effects upon other characters or events.	**B2: Classifications** — Students will be able to categorize different aspects of the text or identify and sort categories from a list of topics or details.	**C2: Inference** — Students will be able to use textual clues to read between the lines and make judgments about specific textual events, ideas, or character analysis.	**D2: Summarizing** — Students will be able to provide a synopsis of text sections.	**E2: Expressing Emotion** — Students will be able to articulate their feelings through a variety of media (e.g., song, art, poem, story, essay, speech).	**F2: Monitoring and Assessing** — Students will be able to analyze a plan of action (including implications, consequences, and big ideas) and articulate future goals to accomplish a task.
Rung 3	**A3: Consequences and Implications** — Students will be able to predict character actions and story outcomes and make real-world forecasts.	**B3: Generalizations** — Students will be able to make general statements about a reading and/or an idea within the reading, using data to support their statements.	**C3: Theme/Concept** — Students will be able to identify a major idea or theme common throughout the text.	**D3: Creative Synthesis** — Students will be able to create something new using what they have learned from the reading and their synopses.	**E3: Using Emotion** — Students will be able to analyze how emotion affects the passage and/or the reader.	**F3: Reflecting** — Students will be able to (a) evaluate ideas and plans, (b) provide new plans of action, and (c) explain the pros/cons of a given selection.

- **Ladder A, Rung 3, Consequences and Implications:** The highest rung on Ladder A requires students to think about both short- and long-term events that may happen as a result of an effect they have identified (e.g., What are the short- and long-term consequences of baking at home?). Students learn to draw consequences and implications from the text for application in the real world.

Ladder B: Focus on Generalizations

The goal of Ladder B is to help students develop deductive reasoning skills, moving from the concrete elements in a story to abstract ideas. Students begin by learning the importance of concrete details and how they can be organized. By the top rung, students are able to make general statements spanning a topic or concept. The rungs are as follows:

- **Ladder B, Rung 1, Details:** The lowest rung on Ladder B, details, requires students to list examples or details from what they have read and/or to list examples they know from the real world or have read about (e.g., Make a list of types of transportation. Write as many as you can think of in 2 minutes).

- **Ladder B, Rung 2, Classifications:** The middle rung of Ladder B, classifications, focuses on students' ability to categorize examples and details based on characteristics (e.g., How might we categorize the modes of transportation you identified?). This activity builds students' skills in categorization and classification.

- **Ladder B, Rung 3, Generalizations:** The highest rung on Ladder B, generalizations, requires students to use the list and categories generated at Rungs 1 and 2 to develop two to three general statements that apply to *all* of their examples (e.g., Write three statements about transportation).

Ladder C: Focus on Themes

The goal of Ladder C is to develop literary analysis skills based on an understanding of literary elements. After completing Ladder C, students state the main themes and ideas of text after identifying the setting, characters, and context of the piece. The rungs for this ladder are as follows:

- **Ladder C, Rung 1, Literary Elements:** While working on the lowest rung of Ladder C, literary elements, students identify and/

or describe the setting or situation in which the reading occurs. This rung also requires students to develop an understanding of a given character by identifying qualities he or she possesses and comparing these qualities to other characters they have encountered in their reading (e.g., In *Goldilocks and the Three Bears*, what is the situation in which Goldilocks finds herself? What qualities do you admire in Goldilocks? What qualities do you find problematic? How is she similar or different from other fairy tale characters you have encountered?).

- **Ladder C, Rung 2, Inference:** Inference serves as the middle rung of Ladder C and requires students to think through a situation in the text and come to a conclusion based on the information and clues provided (e.g., What evidence exists that Goldilocks ate the porridge? What inferences can you make about the bears' subsequent action?).

- **Ladder C, Rung 3, Theme/Concept:** The highest rung of Ladder C, theme/concept, requires students to state the central idea or theme for a reading. This exercise necessitates that the students explain an idea from the reading that best states what the text means (e.g., How would you rename the fairy tale? Why? What is the overall theme of *Goldilocks and the Three Bears*? Which morals apply to the fairy tale? Why?).

Ladder D: Focus on Creative Synthesis

The goal of Ladder D is to help students develop skills in creative synthesis in order to foster students' creation of new material based on information from the reading. It moves from the level of restating ideas to creating new ideas about a topic or concept. The rungs are as follows:

- **Ladder D, Rung 1, Paraphrasing:** The lowest rung on Ladder D is paraphrasing. This rung requires students to restate a short passage using their own words (e.g., Rewrite the following quotation in your own words: "But as soon as [the slave] came near to Androcles, he recognized his friend, and fawned upon him, and licked his hands like a friendly dog. The emperor, surprised at this, summoned Androcles to him, who told the whole story. Whereupon the slave was pardoned and freed, and the Lion let loose to his native forest.").

- **Ladder D, Rung 2, Summarizing:** Summarizing, the middle rung on Ladder D, requires students to summarize larger sections of text by selecting the most important key points within a passage (e.g., Choose one section of the story and summarize it in five sentences).

- **Ladder D, Rung 3, Creative Synthesis:** The highest rung on Ladder D requires students to create something new using what they have learned from the reading and their synopses of it (e.g., Write another fable about the main idea you identified for this fable, using characters, setting, and a plot of your choice).

Ladder E: Focus on Emotional Development

The goal of Ladder E is to help students develop skills in using their emotional intelligence in order to regulate and modulate behavior in respect to learning. It moves from students' understanding of emotion in self and others, to expressing emotion, to channeling emotion for cognitive ends. The rungs are as follows:

- **Ladder E, Rung 1, Understanding Emotion:** The lowest rung on Ladder E is understanding emotion in oneself and others. This requires students to identify emotions in characters and relate it to their own lives (e.g., What feelings does the main character portray throughout the story? How would you compare his temperament to yours?). It also requires them to recognize emotional situations and pinpoint the nature of the emotions involved and what is causing them. Many of the poetry and fiction selections are employed to engage students in the use of this ladder.

- **Ladder E, Rung 2, Expressing Emotion:** The middle rung on Ladder E, expressing emotion, asks students to express emotion in response to their reading of various selections (e.g., The main character seems to worry too much. Is worry ever beneficial? Why or why not?). They may often do this in self-selected formats, including poetry or prose. Teachers may want to substitute kinesthetic responses in the form of dance or skits that demonstrate an emotional reaction to the selections.

- **Ladder E, Rung 3, Using Emotion:** The highest rung on Ladder E, using emotion, encourages students to begin regulating emotion for specific purposes (e.g., How does worry impact your life? What steps can you take to minimize worry? Write a personal action plan). In application to poetry, prose, and biography, students need to demonstrate a clear understanding of how to use emotion effectively for accomplishing specific ends, whether through giving a speech or writing a passionate letter in defense of an idea. The deliberate incorporation of emotion in one's communication is stressed.

Ladder F: Focus on Metacognition

The goal of Ladder F is to help students in planning, monitoring, and evaluating their academic and career goals. Through readings of eminent persons, students examine the impact of various factors that inhibit or enhance personal contributions and trajectories. Then students are asked to apply the new learning to their own individual circumstances and short- and long-term goals. The rungs are as follows:

- **Ladder F, Rung 1, Planning and Goal Setting:** The lowest rung on Ladder F, planning and goal setting, requires students to consider how talented people from all walks of life have deliberately thought about how they will live their lives (e.g., Passion and perseverance are two traits of successful individuals. Describe how this passion and perseverance were evidenced in Bourke-White's life). Through biographical inquiry, students model this behavior in setting their own academic and career goals, based on assessing their interests, aptitudes, and values.

- **Ladder F, Rung 2, Monitoring and Assessing:** The middle rung on Ladder F, monitoring and assessing, requires students to think about their capacity to complete projects and to move forward with goals and outcomes (e.g., What are you passionate about? How can you use that passion for success?). Students are asked to judge the quality of their own products and to assess their own progress toward goals by setting appropriate criteria and then applying them to a situation. By analyzing what eminent individuals have done, students are able to think about the decisions made and the timing of those decisions as they impacted life outcomes.

- **Ladder F, Rung 3, Reflecting:** The highest rung on Ladder F, reflecting, engages students in reflecting on what they have learned from their study of biography and how the principles may apply to their own life planning and career development process (e.g., Write five ways you are successful and five things you need to work on to become more successful. Design a personal growth plan with realistic and achievable goals to become more successful in at least one area of your life). Students are asked to create career plans, to apply the talent development markers to their own lives, and to select the most important aspects of a life for emulation.

Process Skills

Along with the six goals addressed by the ladders, a seventh goal focusing on process skills is incorporated in the *Jacob's Ladder* curriculum. The aim of this goal is to promote learning through interaction and discussion of reading material in the classroom. After completing the ladders and following guidelines for discussion and teacher feedback, students will be able to:

- articulate their understanding of a reading passage using textual support,

- engage in proper dialogue about the meaning of a selection, and

- discuss varied ideas about the intention of a passage both orally and in writing.

Reading Genres and Selections

The reading selections include three major genres: short stories (fables, myths, short stories, and essays), poetry, and nonfiction. In Level 5, each reading within a genre has been carefully selected or tailored for student reading accessibility and interest. The stories and poems for the *Jacob's Ladder* curriculum at each grade level were chosen with three basic criteria in mind: (1) concrete to abstract development, (2) level of vocabulary, and (3) age-appropriate themes. The readings and exercises are designed to move students forward in their abstract thinking processes by promoting critical and creative thinking. The vocabulary in each reading is grade-level appropriate; however, when new or unfamiliar words are encountered, they should be covered in class before the readings and ladder questions are assigned. Themes also are appropriate to the students' ages at each grade level and were chosen to complement themes typically seen in texts for each particular level. The short stories, poetry, and nonfiction readings with corresponding ladder sets are delineated in Part II. Table 2 outlines all Level 5 readings by genre.

TABLE 2
Jacob's Ladder 5 **Selections by Genre**

Short Stories	Poems	Biographies
Mercury and the Sculptor originally told by Aesop	*Ozymandias* by Percy Bysshe Shelley	Ada Lovelace, computer scientist
The Stag at the Pool originally told by Aesop	*The World Is Too Much With Us* by William Wordsworth	Marie Curie, scientist
The Rocking-Horse Winner by D. H. Lawrence	*Ulysses* by Alfred, Lord Tennyson	Emily Dickinson, poet
The Gift of the Magi by O. Henry	*The Lake Isle of Innisfree* by William Butler Yeats	Harriet Tubman, social reformer
The Nightingale and the Rose by Oscar Wilde	*In a Library* by Emily Dickinson	Margaret Mead, anthropologist
The Tell-Tale Heart by Edgar Allen Poe	*Fire and Ice* by Robert Frost	
Ugly by Guy de Maupassant	*We Wear the Mask* by Paul Laurence Dunbar	
A Haunted House by Virginia Woolf		

Rationale

Constructing meaning of the written word is one of the earliest tasks required of students in schools. This skill occupies the central place in the curriculum at the elementary level. Yet, approaches to teaching reading comprehension often are "skill and drill," using worksheets on low-level reading material. As a result, students frequently are unable to transfer these skills from exercise pages and apply them to new, higher level reading material.

The time expended to ensure that students become autonomous and advanced readers would suggest the need for a methodology that deliberately moves students from simple to complex reading skills with grade-appropriate texts. Such a learning approach to reading skill development ensures that students can traverse easily from basic comprehension skills to higher level critical reading skills, while using the same reading stimulus to navigate this transition. Reading comprehension is enhanced by instructional scaffolding, moving students from lower order to higher order thinking, using strategies and processes to help students analyze passages (Villaume & Brabham, 2002). In addition, teachers who emphasize higher order thinking through questions and tasks such as those at the higher rungs of each ladder promote greater reading growth (Taylor, Pearson, Peterson, & Rodriguez, 2003).

Jacob's Ladder was written in response to teacher findings that students needed additional scaffolding to consistently work at higher levels of thinking in reading. This teacher insight is buttressed by findings from cognitive science that suggest that students need to have purpose and direction for discussions of text to yield meaningful learning and that scaffolding is a necessary part of enhancing critical reading behavior (Bransford, Brown, & Cocking, 2000). Similarly, Tivnan and Hemphill (2005) studied reading reform curricula in Title I schools and found that none of the reading programs studied emphasized skills beyond basic phonemic awareness, fluency, or limited comprehension. Therefore, supplementary curriculum that focuses on higher level thinking skills is needed.

The *Jacob's Ladder* program is a compilation of the instructional scaffolding and reading exercises necessary to aid students in their journey toward becoming critical readers. Students learn concept development skills through generalizing, predicting and forecasting skills through delineating implications of events, and literary analysis skills through discerning textual meaning (VanTassel-Baska & Stambaugh, 2006a). The questions and tasks for each reading are open-ended, as this type of approach to responding to literature improves performance on comprehension tests (Guthrie, Schafer, & Huang, 2001). Progressing through the hierarchy of skills also requires students to reread the text, thereby improving metacomprehension accuracy (Rawson, Dunlosky, & Thiede, 2000).

Research Base

A quasi-experimental study was conducted using *Jacob's Ladder* as a supplementary program for grade 3–5 students in Title I schools. After receiving professional development, teachers were instructed to implement the *Jacob's Ladder* curriculum in addition to their basal reading series and guided reading groups.

Findings from this study (N = 495) suggest that when compared to students who used the basal reader only, students who were exposed to the *Jacob's Ladder* curriculum showed significant gains in reading comprehension and critical thinking. Likewise, students who used the curriculum showed significant and important growth on curriculum-based assessments that included determining implications/consequences, making inferences, outlining themes and generalizations, and applying creative synthesis. Students reported greater interest in reading and alluded that the curriculum made them "think harder." Teachers reported more in-depth student discussion and personal growth in their ability to ask open-ended questions in reading (Stambaugh, 2010).

Who Should Use *Jacob's Ladder?*

Although the program is targeted for gifted learners and for promising students who need more exposure to higher level thinking skills in reading, the program may be suitable for other learners as well, including those who are twice-exceptional, students from poverty, and those from different cultural backgrounds (VanTassel-Baska & Stambaugh, 2006b). The reading selections include classic and contemporary literature that has been used at various grade levels with various groups (VanTassel-Baska & Stambaugh, 2006a). The biography material is written at the sixth-grade level and should be high interest for students interested in various careers, especially if they are female or come from different cultural groups as these underrepresented groups comprise the selections of eminent people. The poetry included in Levels 1–3 of the series was written by students of comparable ages who won writing contests.

Implementation Considerations

Teachers need to consider certain issues when implementing the *Jacob's Ladder* curriculum. Because modeling, coaching, and feedback appear to enhance student growth in reading and writing (Pressley et al., 2001; Taylor, Peterson, Pearson, & Rodriquez, 2002), it is recommended that teachers review how to complete the task ladders with the entire class at least once, outlining expectations and record-keeping tasks, as well as modeling the process prior to assigning small-group or independent work. As students gain more confidence in the curriculum, the teacher should allow more independent work coupled with small-group or paired discussion, and then whole-group sharing with teacher feedback.

Completing these activities in dyads or small groups will facilitate discussions that stress collaborative reasoning, thereby fostering greater engagement and higher level thinking (Chin, Anderson, & Waggoner, 2001; Pressley et al., 2001; Taylor et al., 2002). The stories and accompanying ladder questions and activities also may be organized into a reading center in the classroom or utilized with reading groups during guided reading.

Process of *Jacob's Ladder*

The process of inquiry and feedback, as led and modeled by the teacher, is critical to the success of the program and student mastery of process skills. Teachers need to solicit multiple student responses and encourage dialogue about various perspectives and interpretations of a given text, requiring students to justify their answers with textual support and concrete examples (VanTassel-Baska & Stambaugh, 2006a, 2006b). Sample follow-up questions and prompts such as those listed below can be used by the teacher and posted in the classroom to guide student discussion.

- That's interesting; does anyone have a different idea?
- What in the story makes you say that?
- What do you think the author means by . . . ?
- What do you think are the implications or consequences of . . . ?
- Did anyone view that differently? How?
- Does anyone have a different point of view? Justify your answer.
- In the story I noticed that . . . Do you think that might have significance to the overall meaning?
- I heard someone say that they thought the poem (story) was about . . . What do you think? Justify your answer from the events of the story.
- Do you notice any key words that might be significant? Why?
- Do you notice any words that give you a mental picture? Do those words have significance? What might they symbolize?
- I agree with . . . because . . .
- I had a different idea than . . . because . . .

Grouping Students

Jacob's Ladder may be used in a number of different grouping patterns. The program should be introduced initially as a whole-group activity directed by the teacher with appropriate open-ended questions, feedback, and monitoring. After students have examined each type of ladder with teacher guidance, they should be encouraged to use the program by writing ideas independently, sharing with a partner, and then discussing the findings with a group. The dyad approach provides maximal opportunities for student discussion of the readings and collaborative decisions about the answers to questions posed. One purpose of the program is to solicit meaningful discussion of the text, which is best accomplished in small groups of students at similar reading levels (VanTassel-Baska & Little, 2011). Research continues to support instructional grouping in reading as an important part of successful implementation of a program (Rogers, 2002).

Demonstrating Growth: Pre- and Postassessments and Student Products

The pre- and postassessments included in Appendix A were designed as a diagnostic-prescriptive approach to guide program implementation of *Jacob's Ladder*. The pretest should be administered, scored, and then used to guide student instruction and the selection of readings for varied ability groups. Both the pre- and postassessment, scoring rubric, and sample exemplars for each rubric category and level are included in Appendix A along with exemplars to guide scoring.

In both the pre- and postassessments, students read a short passage and respond to the four questions. Question 1 focuses on consequences and implications (Ladder A), Question 2 on generalization, theme, and concept (Ladders B and C), Question 3 on inference (Ladder C), and Question 4 on creative synthesis (Ladder D). By analyzing each question and scored response, teachers may select the appropriate readings and ladders based on student need.

Additionally, in Levels 4 and 5 of the curriculum, a student product is required that assesses the extent to which students can create their own literary selections, using the selections in each book as models and assessing their understanding of Ladders E and F. Emphasis is placed on their ability to plan and organize a creative piece, assess its properties, and reflect on its purpose and audience. Moreover, students are asked to both express an emotion and indicate how it was used in the written piece and for what effect. An assessment rubric accompanies the task demand in each book.

Upon conclusion of the program or as a midpoint check, the posttest may be administered to compare the pretest results and to measure growth in students' responses. These pre-post results could be used as part of a student portfolio, in a parent-teacher conference, or as documentation of curriculum effectiveness and student progress. The pre- and postassessments were piloted to ensure pre-post equivalent forms reliability ($\alpha = .76$) and interrater reliability ($\alpha = .81$).

Student Reflection, Feedback, and Record Keeping

Students may use an answer sheet such as the one provided in Appendix B for each ladder to record their personal thoughts independently before discussing them with a partner. After finishing the ladders for each reading selection, a reflection page (also in Appendix B) can be provided, indicating each student's personal assessment of the work completed. Teachers also will want to check student answers as ladder segments are completed and conduct an individual or small-group consultation to ensure that students understand why their answers may be effective or ineffective. In order to analyze student responses and progress across the program, teachers need to monitor student performance, using the student answer sheets to indicate appropriate completion of tasks. Specific comments about student work also are important to promote growth and understanding of content.

Record-keeping sheets for the class are also provided in Appendix B. On these forms, teachers record student progress on a 3-point scale: 2 (*applies skills very effectively*), 1 (*understands and applies skills*), or 0 (*needs more practice with the given skill set*) across readings and ladder sets. This form can be used as part of a diagnostic-prescriptive approach to selecting reading materials and ladders based on student understanding or the need for more practice.

Sample Concluding Activities: Ideas for Grades

Grading the ladders and responses are at the teacher's discretion. Teachers should not overemphasize the lower rungs in graded activities. Lower rungs are intended only as a vehicle to the higher level questions at the top of the ladder. Instead, top-rung questions may be used as a journal prompt or as part of a graded, open-ended writing response. Grades also could be given based on guided discussion after students are trained on appropriate ways to discuss literature. Additional ideas for grading are as follows:

- Write a persuasive essay to justify what you think the story is about.

- Create a symbol to show the meaning of the story. Write two sentences to justify your symbol.

- In one word or phrase, what is this story mostly about? Justify your answer using examples from the story.

- Write a letter from the author's point of view, explaining what the meaning of the story is to young children.

- Pretend you are an illustrator and need to create a drawing for the story or poem that shows what the story or poem is mostly about. Write a sentence to describe your illustration and why it is the best option.

- You have been reading biographies of eminent people in many fields. Select one and act out a scene from the person's life as you imagine it.

- The importance of emotion in storytelling cannot be overstressed. Analyze a favorite story according to its emotional content and how it contributed to your liking the story.

Time Allotment

Although the time needed to complete *Jacob's Ladder* tasks will vary by student, most lessons should take students 15–30 minutes to read the selection and another 15–20 minutes to complete one ladder individually. More time is required for paired student and whole-group discussion of the questions. Teachers may wish to set aside 2 days each week for focusing on one *Jacob's Ladder* reading and its commensurate ladders, especially when introducing the program.

Answer Sets

Because the questions for Ladders E and F are highly individualized and open-ended, no answer sets are given in Levels 4 and 5 of the program. Also, students in grades 7–9 should be encouraged to seek out the levels of meaning in rich text, looking for multiple answers that reflect their own experience.

Alignment to Standards

Appendix C contains alignment charts to demonstrate the connection of the fiction and nonfiction reading materials to relevant national standards. One of the benefits of this program is its ability to provide cross-disciplinary coverage of standards through the use of a single reading stimulus. Connections to science and social studies standards are noted. Alignment to the new national standards in English/language arts have been used as the basis for the analysis.

References

Bransford, J. D., Brown, A. L., & Cocking, R. R. (2000). *How people learn: Brain, mind, experience.* Washington, DC: National Academy Press.

Chin, C. A., Anderson, R. C., & Waggoner, M. A. (2001). Patterns of discourse in two kinds of literature discussion. *Reading Research Quarterly, 30,* 378–411.

Guthrie, J. T., Schafer, W. D., & Huang, C. (2001). Benefits of opportunity to read and balanced instruction on the NAEP. *Journal of Educational Research, 94,* 145–162.

Pressley, M., Wharton-McDonald, R., Allington, R., Block, C. C., Morrow, L., Tracey, D., . . . Woo, D. (2001). A study of effective first-grade literacy instruction. *Scientific Studies of Reading, 5,* 35–58.

Rawson, K. A., Dunlosky, J., & Thiede, K. W. (2000). The rereading effect: Metacomprehension accuracy improves across reading trials. *Memory & Cognition, 28*(6), 1004.

Rogers, K. (2002). *Re-forming gifted education: How parents and teachers can match the program to the child.* Scottsdale, AZ: Great Potential Press.

Stambaugh, T. (2010). *Effects of the Jacob's Ladder Reading Comprehension Program.* Manuscript submitted for publication.

Taylor, B. M., Pearson, P. D., Peterson, D. S., & Rodriguez, M. C. (2003). Reading growth in high-poverty classrooms: The influence of teacher practices that encourage cognitive engagement in literacy learning. *The Elementary School Journal, 104,* 3–30.

Taylor, B. M., Peterson, D. P., Pearson, P. D., & Rodriguez, M. C. (2002). Looking inside classrooms: Reflecting on the "how" as well as the "what" in effective reading instruction. *Reading Teacher, 56,* 270–279.

Tivnan, T., & Hemphill, L. (2005). Comparing four literacy reform models in high-poverty schools: Patterns of first grade achievement. *Elementary School Journal, 105,* 419–443.

VanTassel-Baska, J., & Stambaugh, T. (2006a). *Comprehensive curriculum for gifted learners* (3rd ed.). Needham Heights, MA: Allyn & Bacon.

VanTassel-Baska, J., & Stambaugh, T. (2006b). Project Athena: A pathway to advanced literacy development for children of poverty. *Gifted Child Today, 29*(2), 58–65.

VanTassel-Baska, J., & Little, C. (Eds.). (2011). *Content-based curriculum for gifted learners* (2nd ed.). Waco, TX: Prufrock Press.

Villaume, S. K., & Brabham, E. G. (2002). Comprehension instruction: Beyond strategies. *The Reading Teacher, 55,* 672–676.

Part II: Readings and Student Ladder Sets

CHAPTER 1

Short Stories

Chapter 1: Short Stories

Chapter 1 includes the selected readings and accompanying question sets for each fable or short story selection. Each reading is followed by three or four sets of questions; each set is aligned to one of the six sets of ladder skills.

For *Jacob's Ladder 5*, the skills covered by each selection are as follows:

Title	Ladder Skills
Mercury and the Sculptor	C, D, E
The Stag at the Pool	A, B, C, F
The Rocking-Horse Winner	A, C, D
The Gift of the Magi	C, D, E
The Nightingale and the Rose	A, C, E
The Tell-Tale Heart	C, D, E
Ugly	B, D, E
A Haunted House	A, C, D

Mercury and the Sculptor
Originally told by Aesop

Mercury was very anxious to know in what estimation he was held by mankind, so he disguised himself as a man and walked into a sculptor's studio where there were a number of statues finished and ready for sale. Seeing a statue of Jupiter among the rest, he inquired the price of it. "A crown," said the Sculptor. "Is that all?" said he, laughing. "And (pointing to one of Juno) how much is that one?" "That," was the reply, "is half a crown." "And how much might you be wanting for that one over there, now?" he continued, pointing to a statue of himself. "That one?" said the sculptor. "Oh, I'll throw him in for nothing if you'll buy the other two."

Theme/Concept

C3

What is the main idea or theme of this fable?
Write your own moral for it.

Inference

C2

Why might the sculptor have decided to include the third statue for the same price? Cite three possibilities. What would Mercury have inferred to be the reason the sculptor did it?

Literary Elements

C1

What human characteristics does Mercury show?

MERCURY AND THE SCULPTOR

D3

Creative Synthesis

Create a fable containing two characters, a situation where one wants to acquire information from the other, and the use of disguise. State your moral.

Summarizing

D2

Summarize the story from Mercury's point of view.

Paraphrasing

D1

Paraphrase the response of the sculptor. What do you think he is really saying?

MERCURY AND THE SCULPTOR

Using Emotion

E3

How could you use your feelings in such a situation to improve your standing with the sculptor? Write about a time when you were hurt by someone's unintentional comments. What did you learn from that experience?

Expressing Emotion

E2

What would have been your response to the sculptor?

Understanding Emotion

E1

Put yourself in Mercury's winged shoes. How would you feel if the sculptor had spoken to you as he did to Mercury?

MERCURY AND THE SCULPTOR

The Stag at the Pool
Originally told by Aesop

A Stag overpowered by heat came to a spring to drink. Seeing his own shadow reflected in the water, he greatly admired the size and variety of his horns, but felt angry with himself for having such slender and weak feet. While he was thus contemplating himself, a Lion appeared at the pool and crouched to spring upon him. The Stag immediately took to flight, and exerting his utmost speed, as long as the plain was smooth and open, kept himself easily at a safe distance from the Lion. But entering a wood he became entangled by his horns, and the Lion quickly came up to him and caught him. When too late, he thus reproached himself: "Woe is me! How I have deceived myself! These feet which would have saved me I despised, and I gloried in these antlers which have proved my destruction."

What is most truly valuable is often underrated.

Name: _____ Date: _____

Consequences and Implications

A3

What are the implications of focusing only on assets
and not liabilities when you make decisions?

Cause and Effect

A2

How did the stag's asset become his liability? Describe a time
when your best asset also became a liability for you.

Sequencing

A1

What would have happened if the stag had not gone into the woods?

THE STAG AT THE POOL

Generalizations

B3

What are some traits that humans develop that help them live a full and long life? Based on your understanding of these traits, both positive and negative, what generalizations can you make about what causes happiness? What causes unhappiness?

Classifications

B2

How would you categorize these traits?

Details

B1

Provide examples of other human traits that can cause problems in living a full and long life.

THE STAG AT THE POOL

Theme/Concept

C3

Create a story about another animal or person that
has a moral similar to the one in this story.

Inference

C2

What does the moral of the fable (refer to the last line) mean?

Literary Elements

C1

What human characteristics did the stag show?
Why was he upset with himself?

THE STAG AT THE POOL

Reflecting

F3

Based on your planning guide and your assessment of recent experiences, what career seems to be the most appealing to you and why? What careers would you like to know more about? What will you do to get more career guidance?

Monitoring and Assessing

F2

Using the chart on page 31, assess your experiences (academic, personal, or other) over the past year. Choose three experiences to describe in respect to how they have moved you toward a career path. What about the experience impacted your thinking about a career? How did the experience make you feel? Evaluate each experience according to its importance in moving you toward a career (1 is low, 5 is high).

Planning and Goal Setting

F1

Knowing one's assets and liabilities is a useful tool in career planning as well as in escaping lions. Complete the activities on page 32 based on your understanding of the story's moral.

Create a planning guide for careers that plots your interests, your assets that would allow you to perform well in the career, your liabilities that may hold you back, and the benefits you see for yourself in the career. Choose three careers from the following list for your self-analysis: doctor, lawyer, computer specialist, writer, graphic designer, teacher, hotel manager, public relations agent, or financial planner.

THE STAG AT THE POOL

Name: _____ Date: _____

THE STAG AT THE POOL
Monitoring and Assessing

Assess your experiences (academic, personal, or other) over the past year. Choose three experiences to describe in respect to how they have moved you toward a career path. What about the experience impacted your thinking about a career? How did the experience make you feel? Evaluate each experience according to its importance in moving you toward a career (1 is low, 5 is high).

	Experience	Impact on Thinking About Career	Feelings	Rating of Experience
1.				
2.				
3.				

Name: _____   Date: _____

THE STAG AT THE POOL
Planning and Goal Setting

Knowing one's assets and liabilities is a useful tool in career planning as well as in escaping lions. Complete the following activities based on your understanding of the story's moral.

Using the chart below, create a planning guide for careers that plots your interests, your assets that would allow you to perform well in the career, your liabilities that may hold you back, and the benefits you see for yourself in the career. Choose three careers from the following list for your self-analysis: doctor, lawyer, computer specialist, writer, graphic designer, teacher, hotel manager, public relations agent, or financial planner.

Planning Guide				
Career Choice	Interest Indicators	Skills and Assets	Liabilities	Benefits

The Rocking-Horse Winner
by D. H. Lawrence

There was a woman who was beautiful, who started with all the advantages, yet she had no luck. She married for love, and the love turned to dust. She had bonny children, yet she felt they had been thrust upon her, and she could not love them. They looked at her coldly, as if they were finding fault with her. And hurriedly she felt she must cover up some fault in herself. Yet what it was that she must cover up she never knew. Nevertheless, when her children were present, she always felt the centre of her heart go hard. This troubled her, and in her manner she was all the more gentle and anxious for her children, as if she loved them very much. Only she herself knew that at the centre of her heart was a hard little place that could not feel love, no, not for anybody. Everybody else said of her: "She is such a good mother. She adores her children." Only she herself, and her children themselves, knew it was not so. They read it in each other's eyes.

There were a boy and two little girls. They lived in a pleasant house, with a garden, and they had discreet servants, and felt themselves superior to anyone in the neighbourhood.

Although they lived in style, they felt always an anxiety in the house. There was never enough money. The mother had a small income, and the father had a small income, but not nearly enough for the social position which they had to keep up. The father went into town to some office. But though he had good prospects, these prospects never materialised. There was always the grinding sense of the shortage of money, though the style was always kept up.

At last the mother said: "I will see if I can't make something." But she did not know where to begin. She racked her brains, and tried this thing and the other, but could not find anything successful. The failure made deep lines come into her face. Her children were growing up, they would have to go to school. There must be more money, there must be more money. The father, who was always very handsome and expensive in his tastes, seemed as if he never would be able to do anything worth doing. And the mother, who had a great belief in herself, did not succeed any better, and her tastes were just as expensive.

And so the house came to be haunted by the unspoken phrase: There must be more money! There must be more money! The children could hear it all the time though nobody said it aloud. They heard it at Christmas, when the expensive and splendid toys filled the nursery. Behind the shining modern rocking-horse, behind the smart doll's house, a voice would start whispering: "There must be more money! There must be more money!" And the children would stop playing, to listen for a moment. They would look into each other's eyes, to see if they had all heard. And each one saw in the eyes of the other two that they too had heard. "There must be more money! There must be more money!"

It came whispering from the springs of the still-swaying rocking-horse, and even the horse, bending his wooden, champing head, heard it. The big doll, sitting so pink and smirking in her new pram, could hear it quite plainly, and seemed to be smirking all the more self-consciously because of it. The foolish puppy, too, that took the place of the teddy-bear, he was looking so extraordinarily foolish for no other reason but that he heard the secret whisper all over the house: "There must be more money!"

Yet nobody ever said it aloud. The whisper was everywhere, and therefore no one spoke it. Just as no one ever says: "We are breathing!" in spite of the fact that breath is coming and going all the time.

"Mother," said the boy Paul one day, "why don't we keep a car of our own? Why do we always use uncle's, or else a taxi?"

"Because we're the poor members of the family," said the mother.

"But why are we, mother?"

"Well—I suppose," she said slowly and bitterly, "it's because your father has no luck."

The boy was silent for some time.

"Is luck money, mother?" he asked, rather timidly.

"No, Paul. Not quite. It's what causes you to have money."

"Oh!" said Paul vaguely. "I thought when Uncle Oscar said filthy lucker, it meant money."

"Filthy lucre does mean money," said the mother. "But it's lucre, not luck."

"Oh!" said the boy. "Then what is luck, mother?"

"It's what causes you to have money. If you're lucky you have money. That's why it's better to be born lucky than rich. If you're rich, you may lose your money. But if you're lucky, you will always get more money."

"Oh! Will you? And is father not lucky?"

"Very unlucky, I should say," she said bitterly.

The boy watched her with unsure eyes.

"Why?" he asked.

"I don't know. Nobody ever knows why one person is lucky and another unlucky."

"Don't they? Nobody at all? Does nobody know?"

"Perhaps God. But He never tells."

"He ought to, then. And aren't you lucky either, mother?"

"I can't be, if I married an unlucky husband."

"But by yourself, aren't you?"

"I used to think I was, before I married. Now I think I am very unlucky indeed."

"Why?"

"Well—never mind! Perhaps I'm not really," she said.

The child looked at her to see if she meant it. But he saw, by the lines of her mouth, that she was only trying to hide something from him.

"Well, anyhow," he said stoutly, "I'm a lucky person."

"Why?" said his mother, with a sudden laugh.

He stared at her. He didn't even know why he had said it.

"God told me," he asserted, brazening it out.

"I hope He did, dear!", she said, again with a laugh, but rather bitter.

"He did, mother!"

"Excellent!" said the mother, using one of her husband's exclamations.

The boy saw she did not believe him; or rather, that she paid no attention to his assertion. This angered him somewhere, and made him want to compel her attention.

He went off by himself, vaguely, in a childish way, seeking for the clue to "luck." Absorbed, taking no heed of other people, he went about with a sort of stealth, seeking inwardly for luck. He wanted luck, he wanted it, he wanted it. When the two girls were playing dolls in the nursery, he would sit on his big rocking-horse, charging madly into space, with a frenzy that made the little girls peer at him uneasily. Wildly the horse careered, the waving dark hair of the boy tossed, his eyes had a strange glare in them. The little girls dared not speak to him.

When he had ridden to the end of his mad little journey, he climbed down and stood in front of his rocking-horse, staring fixedly into its lowered face. Its red mouth was slightly open, its big eye was wide and glassy-bright.

"Now!" he would silently command the snorting steed. "Now take me to where there is luck! Now take me!"

And he would slash the horse on the neck with the little whip he had asked Uncle Oscar for. He knew the horse could take him to where there was luck, if only he forced it. So he would mount again and start on his furious ride, hoping at last to get there.

"You'll break your horse, Paul!" said the nurse.

"He's always riding like that! I wish he'd leave off!" said his elder sister Joan.

But he only glared down on them in silence. Nurse gave him up. She could make nothing of him. Anyhow, he was growing beyond her.

One day his mother and his Uncle Oscar came in when he was on one of his furious rides. He did not speak to them.

"Hallo, you young jockey! Riding a winner?" said his uncle.

"Aren't you growing too big for a rocking-horse? You're not a very little boy any longer, you know," said his mother.

But Paul only gave a blue glare from his big, rather close-set eyes. He would speak to nobody when he was in full tilt. His mother watched him with an anxious expression on her face.

At last he suddenly stopped forcing his horse into the mechanical gallop and slid down.

"Well, I got there!" he announced fiercely, his blue eyes still flaring, and his sturdy long legs straddling apart.

"Where did you get to?" asked his mother.

"Where I wanted to go," he flared back at her.

"That's right, son!" said Uncle Oscar. "Don't you stop till you get there. What's the horse's name?"

"He doesn't have a name," said the boy.

"Get's on without all right?" asked the uncle.

"Well, he has different names. He was called Sansovino last week."

"Sansovino, eh? Won the Ascot. How did you know this name?"

"He always talks about horse-races with Bassett," said Joan.

The uncle was delighted to find that his small nephew was posted with all the racing news. Bassett, the young gardener, who had been wounded in the left foot in the war and had got his present job through Oscar Cresswell, whose batman he had been, was a perfect blade of the "turf." He lived in the racing events, and the small boy lived with him.

Oscar Cresswell got it all from Bassett.

"Master Paul comes and asks me, so I can't do more than tell him, sir," said Bassett, his face terribly serious, as if he were speaking of religious matters.

"And does he ever put anything on a horse he fancies?"

"Well—I don't want to give him away—he's a young sport, a fine sport, sir. Would you mind asking him himself? He sort of takes a pleasure in it, and perhaps he'd feel I was giving him away, sir, if you don't mind."

Bassett was serious as a church.

The uncle went back to his nephew and took him off for a ride in the car.

"Say, Paul, old man, do you ever put anything on a horse?" the uncle asked.

The boy watched the handsome man closely.

"Why, do you think I oughtn't to?" he parried.

"Not a bit of it! I thought perhaps you might give me a tip for the Lincoln."

The car sped on into the country, going down to Uncle Oscar's place in Hampshire.

"Honour bright?" said the nephew.

"Honour bright, son!" said the uncle.

"Well, then, Daffodil."

"Daffodil! I doubt it, sonny. What about Mirza?"

"I only know the winner," said the boy. "That's Daffodil."

"Daffodil, eh?"

There was a pause. Daffodil was an obscure horse comparatively.

"Uncle!"

"Yes, son?"

"You won't let it go any further, will you? I promised Bassett."

"Bassett be damned, old man! What's he got to do with it?"

"We're partners. We've been partners from the first. Uncle, he lent me my first five shillings, which I lost. I promised him, honour bright, it was only between me and him; only you gave me that ten-shilling note I started winning with, so I thought you were lucky. You won't let it go any further, will you?"

The boy gazed at his uncle from those big, hot, blue eyes, set rather close together. The uncle stirred and laughed uneasily.

"Right you are, son! I'll keep your tip private. How much are you putting on him?"

"All except twenty pounds," said the boy. "I keep that in reserve."

The uncle thought it a good joke.

"You keep twenty pounds in reserve, do you, you young romancer? What are you betting, then?"

"I'm betting three hundred," said the boy gravely. "But it's between you and me, Uncle Oscar! Honour bright?"

"It's between you and me all right, you young Nat Gould," he said, laughing. "But where's your three hundred?"

"Bassett keeps it for me. We're partners."

"You are, are you! And what is Bassett putting on Daffodil?"

"He won't go quite as high as I do, I expect. Perhaps he'll go a hundred and fifty."

"What, pennies?" laughed the uncle.

"Pounds," said the child, with a surprised look at his uncle. "Bassett keeps a bigger reserve than I do."

Between wonder and amusement Uncle Oscar was silent. He pursued the matter no further, but he determined to take his nephew with him to the Lincoln races.

"Now, son," he said, "I'm putting twenty on Mirza, and I'll put five on for you on any horse you fancy. What's your pick?"

"Daffodil, uncle."

"No, not the fiver on Daffodil!"

"I should if it was my own fiver," said the child.

"Good! Good! Right you are! A fiver for me and a fiver for you on Daffodil."

The child had never been to a race-meeting before, and his eyes were blue fire. He pursed his mouth tight and watched. A Frenchman just in front had put his money on Lancelot. Wild with excitement, he flayed his arms up and down, yelling "Lancelot!, Lancelot!" in his French accent.

Daffodil came in first, Lancelot second, Mirza third. The child, flushed and with eyes blazing, was curiously serene. His uncle brought him four five-pound notes, four to one.

"What am I to do with these?" he cried, waving them before the boy's eyes.

"I suppose we'll talk to Bassett," said the boy. "I expect I have fifteen hundred now; and twenty in reserve; and this twenty."

His uncle studied him for some moments.

"Look here, son!" he said. "You're not serious about Bassett and that fifteen hundred, are you?"

"Yes, I am. But it's between you and me, uncle. Honour bright?"

"Honour bright all right, son! But I must talk to Bassett."

"If you'd like to be a partner, uncle, with Bassett and me, we could all be partners. Only, you'd have to promise, honour bright, uncle, not to let it go beyond us three. Bassett and I are lucky, and you must be lucky, because it was your ten shillings I started winning with . . ."

Uncle Oscar took both Bassett and Paul into Richmond Park for an afternoon, and there they talked.

"It's like this, you see, sir," Bassett said. "Master Paul would get me talking about racing events, spinning yarns, you know, sir. And he was always keen on knowing if I'd made or if I'd lost. It's about a year since, now, that I put five shillings on Blush of Dawn for him: and we lost. Then the luck turned, with that ten shillings he had from you: that we put on Singhalese. And since that time, it's been pretty steady, all things considering. What do you say, Master Paul?"

"We're all right when we're sure," said Paul. "It's when we're not quite sure that we go down."

"Oh, but we're careful then," said Bassett.

"But when are you sure?" smiled Uncle Oscar.

"It's Master Paul, sir," said Bassett in a secret, religious voice. "It's as if he had it from heaven. Like Daffodil, now, for the Lincoln. That was as sure as eggs."

"Did you put anything on Daffodil?" asked Oscar Cresswell.

"Yes, sir, I made my bit."

"And my nephew?"

Bassett was obstinately silent, looking at Paul.

"I made twelve hundred, didn't I, Bassett? I told uncle I was putting three hundred on Daffodil."

"That's right," said Bassett, nodding.

"But where's the money?" asked the uncle.

"I keep it safe locked up, sir. Master Paul he can have it any minute he likes to ask for it."

"What, fifteen hundred pounds?"

"And twenty! And forty, that is, with the twenty he made on the course."

"It's amazing!" said the uncle.

"If Master Paul offers you to be partners, sir, I would, if I were you: if you'll excuse me," said Bassett.

Oscar Cresswell thought about it.

"I'll see the money," he said.

They drove home again, and, sure enough, Bassett came round to the garden-house with fifteen hundred pounds in notes. The twenty pounds reserve was left with Joe Glee, in the Turf Commission deposit.

"You see, it's all right, uncle, when I'm sure! Then we go strong, for all we're worth, don't we, Bassett?"

"We do that, Master Paul."

"And when are you sure?" said the uncle, laughing.

"Oh, well, sometimes I'm absolutely sure, like about Daffodil," said the boy; "and sometimes I have an idea; and sometimes I haven't even an idea, have I, Bassett? Then we're careful, because we mostly go down."

"You do, do you! And when you're sure, like about Daffodil, what makes you sure, sonny?"

"Oh, well, I don't know," said the boy uneasily. "I'm sure, you know, uncle; that's all."

"It's as if he had it from heaven, sir," Bassett reiterated.

"I should say so!" said the uncle.

But he became a partner. And when the Leger was coming on Paul was "sure" about Lively Spark, which was a quite inconsiderable horse. The boy insisted on putting a thousand on the horse, Bassett went for five hundred, and Oscar Cresswell two hundred. Lively Spark came in first, and the betting had been ten to one against him. Paul had made ten thousand.

"You see," he said. "I was absolutely sure of him."

Even Oscar Cresswell had cleared two thousand.

"Look here, son," he said, "this sort of thing makes me nervous."

"It needn't, uncle! Perhaps I shan't be sure again for a long time."

"But what are you going to do with your money?" asked the uncle.

"Of course," said the boy, "I started it for mother. She said she had no luck, because father is unlucky, so I thought if I was lucky, it might stop whispering."

"What might stop whispering?"

"Our house. I hate our house for whispering."

"What does it whisper?"

"Why - why"—the boy fidgeted—"why, I don't know. But it's always short of money, you know, uncle."

"I know it, son, I know it."

"You know people send mother writs, don't you, uncle?"

"I'm afraid I do," said the uncle.

"And then the house whispers, like people laughing at you behind your back. It's awful, that is! I thought if I was lucky—"

"You might stop it," added the uncle.

The boy watched him with big blue eyes, that had an uncanny cold fire in them, and he said never a word.

"Well, then!" said the uncle. "What are we doing?"

"I shouldn't like mother to know I was lucky," said the boy.

"Why not, son?"

"She'd stop me."

"I don't think she would."

"Oh!"—and the boy writhed in an odd way—"I don't want her to know, uncle."

"All right, son! We'll manage it without her knowing."

They managed it very easily. Paul, at the other's suggestion, handed over five thousand pounds to his uncle, who deposited it with the family lawyer, who was then to inform Paul's mother that a relative had put five thousand pounds into his hands, which sum was to be paid out a thousand pounds at a time, on the mother's birthday, for the next five years.

"So she'll have a birthday present of a thousand pounds for five successive years," said Uncle Oscar. "I hope it won't make it all the harder for her later."

Paul's mother had her birthday in November. The house had been "whispering" worse than ever lately, and, even in spite of his luck, Paul could not bear up against it. He was very anxious to see the effect of the birthday letter, telling his mother about the thousand pounds.

When there were no visitors, Paul now took his meals with his parents, as he was beyond the nursery control. His mother went into town nearly every day. She had discovered that she had an odd knack of sketching furs and dress materials, so she worked secretly in the studio of a friend who was the chief "artist" for the leading drapers. She drew the figures of ladies in furs and ladies in silk and sequins for the newspaper advertisements. This young woman artist earned several thousand pounds a year, but Paul's mother only made several hundreds, and she was again dissatisfied. She so wanted to be first in something, and she did not succeed, even in making sketches for drapery advertisements.

She was down to breakfast on the morning of her birthday. Paul watched her face as she read her letters. He knew the lawyer's letter. As his mother read it, her face hardened and became more expressionless. Then a cold, determined look came on her mouth. She hid the letter under the pile of others, and said not a word about it.

"Didn't you have anything nice in the post for your birthday, mother?" said Paul.

"Quite moderately nice," she said, her voice cold and hard and absent.

She went away to town without saying more.

But in the afternoon Uncle Oscar appeared. He said Paul's mother had had a long interview with the lawyer, asking if the whole five thousand could not be advanced at once, as she was in debt.

"What do you think, uncle?" said the boy.

"I leave it to you, son."

"Oh, let her have it, then! We can get some more with the other," said the boy.

"A bird in the hand is worth two in the bush, laddie!" said Uncle Oscar.

"But I'm sure to know for the Grand National; or the Lincolnshire; or else the Derby. I'm sure to know for one of them," said Paul.

So Uncle Oscar signed the agreement, and Paul's mother touched the whole five thousand. Then something very curious happened. The voices in the house suddenly went mad, like a chorus of frogs on a spring evening. There were certain new furnishings, and Paul had a tutor. He was really going to Eton, his father's school, in the following autumn. There were flowers in the winter, and a blossoming of the luxury Paul's mother had been used to. And yet the voices in the house, behind the sprays of mimosa and almond-blossom, and from under the piles of iridescent cushions, simply trilled and screamed in a sort of ecstasy: "There must be more money! Oh-h-h; there must be more money. Oh, now, now-w! Now-w-w—there must be more money!—more than ever! More than ever!"

It frightened Paul terribly. He studied away at his Latin and Greek with his tutor. But his intense hours were spent with Bassett. The Grand National had gone by: he had not "known," and had lost a hundred pounds. Summer was at hand. He was in agony for the Lincoln. But even for the Lincoln he didn't "know," and he lost fifty pounds. He became wild-eyed and strange, as if something were going to explode in him.

"Let it alone, son! Don't you bother about it!" urged Uncle Oscar. But it was as if the boy couldn't really hear what his uncle was saying.

"I've got to know for the Derby! I've got to know for the Derby!" the child reiterated, his big blue eyes blazing with a sort of madness.

His mother noticed how overwrought he was.

"You'd better go to the seaside. Wouldn't you like to go now to the seaside, instead of waiting? I think you'd better," she said, looking down at him anxiously, her heart curiously heavy because of him.

But the child lifted his uncanny blue eyes.

"I couldn't possibly go before the Derby, mother!" he said. "I couldn't possibly!"

"Why not?" she said, her voice becoming heavy when she was opposed. "Why not? You can still go from the seaside to see the Derby with your Uncle Oscar, if that that's what you wish. No need for you to wait here. Besides, I think you care too much about these races. It's a bad sign. My family has been a gambling family, and you won't know till you grow up how much damage it has done. But it has done damage. I shall have to send Bassett away, and ask Uncle Oscar not to talk racing to you, unless you promise to be reasonable about it: go away to the seaside and forget it. You're all nerves!"

"I'll do what you like, mother, so long as you don't send me away till after the Derby," the boy said.

"Send you away from where? Just from this house?"

"Yes," he said, gazing at her.

"Why, you curious child, what makes you care about this house so much, suddenly? I never knew you loved it."

He gazed at her without speaking. He had a secret within a secret, something he had not divulged, even to Bassett or to his Uncle Oscar.

But his mother, after standing undecided and a little bit sullen for some moments, said: "Very well, then! Don't go to the seaside till after the Derby, if you don't wish it. But promise me you won't think so much about horse-racing and events as you call them!"

"Oh no," said the boy casually. "I won't think much about them, mother. You needn't worry. I wouldn't worry, mother, if I were you."

"If you were me and I were you," said his mother, "I wonder what we should do!"

"But you know you needn't worry, mother, don't you?" the boy repeated.

"I should be awfully glad to know it," she said wearily.

"Oh, well, you can, you know. I mean, you ought to know you needn't worry," he insisted.

"Ought I? Then I'll see about it," she said.

Paul's secret of secrets was his wooden horse, that which had no name. Since he was emancipated from a nurse and a nursery-governess, he had had his rocking-horse removed to his own bedroom at the top of the house.

"Surely you're too big for a rocking-horse!" his mother had remonstrated.

"Well, you see, mother, till I can have a real horse, I like to have some sort of animal about," had been his quaint answer.

"Do you feel he keeps you company?" she laughed.

"Oh yes! He's very good, he always keeps me company, when I'm there," said Paul.

So the horse, rather shabby, stood in an arrested prance in the boy's bedroom.

The Derby was drawing near, and the boy grew more and more tense. He hardly heard what was spoken to him, he was very frail, and his eyes were really uncanny. His mother had sudden strange seizures of uneasiness about him. Sometimes, for half an hour, she would feel a sudden anxiety about him that was almost anguish. She wanted to rush to him at once, and know he was safe.

Two nights before the Derby, she was at a big party in town, when one of her rushes of anxiety about her boy, her first-born, gripped her heart till she could hardly speak. She fought with the feeling, might and main, for she believed in common sense. But it was too strong. She had to leave the dance and go downstairs to telephone to the country. The children's nursery-governess was terribly surprised and startled at being rung up in the night.

"Are the children all right, Miss Wilmot?"

"Oh yes, they are quite all right."

"Master Paul? Is he all right?"

"He went to bed as right as a trivet. Shall I run up and look at him?"

"No," said Paul's mother reluctantly. "No! Don't trouble. It's all right. Don't sit up. We shall be home fairly soon." She did not want her son's privacy intruded upon.

"Very good," said the governess.

It was about one o'clock when Paul's mother and father drove up to their house. All was still. Paul's mother went to her room and slipped off her white fur cloak. She had told her maid not to wait up for her. She heard her husband downstairs, mixing a whisky and soda.

And then, because of the strange anxiety at her heart, she stole upstairs to her son's room. Noiselessly she went along the upper corridor. Was there a faint noise? What was it?

She stood, with arrested muscles, outside his door, listening. There was a strange, heavy, and yet not loud noise. Her heart stood still. It was a soundless noise, yet rushing and powerful. Something huge, in violent, hushed motion. What was it? What in God's name was it? She ought to know. She felt that she knew the noise. She knew what it was.

Yet she could not place it. She couldn't say what it was. And on and on it went, like a madness.

Softly, frozen with anxiety and fear, she turned the door-handle.

The room was dark. Yet in the space near the window, she heard and saw something plunging to and fro. She gazed in fear and amazement.

Then suddenly she switched on the light, and saw her son, in his green pajamas, madly surging on the rocking-horse. The blaze of light suddenly lit him up, as he urged the wooden horse, and lit her up, as she stood, blonde, in her dress of pale green and crystal, in the doorway.

"Paul!" she cried. "Whatever are you doing?"

"It's Malabar!" he screamed in a powerful, strange voice. "It's Malabar!"

His eyes blazed at her for one strange and senseless second, as he ceased urging his wooden horse. Then he fell with a crash to the ground, and she, all her tormented motherhood flooding upon her, rushed to gather him up.

But he was unconscious, and unconscious he remained, with some brain-fever. He talked and tossed, and his mother sat stonily by his side.

"Malabar! It's Malabar! Bassett, Bassett, I know! It's Malabar!"

So the child cried, trying to get up and urge the rocking-horse that gave him his inspiration.

"What does he mean by Malabar?" asked the heart-frozen mother.

"I don't know," said the father stonily.

"What does he mean by Malabar?" she asked her brother Oscar.

"It's one of the horses running for the Derby," was the answer.

And, in spite of himself, Oscar Cresswell spoke to Bassett, and himself put a thousand on Malabar: at fourteen to one.

The third day of the illness was critical: they were waiting for a change. The boy, with his rather long, curly hair, was tossing ceaselessly on the pillow. He neither slept nor regained consciousness, and his eyes were like blue stones. His mother sat, feeling her heart had gone, turned actually into a stone.

In the evening Oscar Cresswell did not come, but Bassett sent a message, saying could he come up for one moment, just one moment? Paul's mother was very angry at the intrusion, but on second thoughts she agreed. The boy was the same. Perhaps Bassett might bring him to consciousness.

The gardener, a shortish fellow with a little brown moustache and sharp little brown eyes, tiptoed into the room, touched his imaginary cap to Paul's mother, and stole to the bedside, staring with glittering, smallish eyes at the tossing, dying child.

"Master Paul!" he whispered. "Master Paul! Malabar came in first all right, a clean win. I did as you told me. You've made over seventy thousand pounds, you have; you've got over eighty thousand. Malabar came in all right, Master Paul."

"Malabar! Malabar! Did I say Malabar, mother? Did I say Malabar? Do you think I'm lucky, mother? I knew Malabar, didn't I? Over eighty thousand pounds! I call that lucky, don't you, mother? Over eighty thousand pounds! I knew, didn't I know I knew? Malabar came in all right. If I ride my horse till I'm sure, then I tell you, Bassett, you can go as high as you like. Did you go for all you were worth, Bassett?"

"I went a thousand on it, Master Paul."

"I never told you, mother, that if I can ride my horse, and get there, then I'm absolutely sure —oh, absolutely! Mother, did I ever tell you? I am lucky!"

"No, you never did," said his mother.

But the boy died in the night.

And even as he lay dead, his mother heard her brother's voice saying to her, "My God, Hester, you're eighty-odd thousand to the good, and a poor devil of a son to the bad. But, poor devil, poor devil, he's best gone out of a life where he rides his rocking-horse to find a winner."

THE ROCKING-HORSE WINNER

Consequences and Implications

A3

What are the implications of Hester's greed on her son?

Cause and Effect

A2

What causes the major conflict in the story? How does it impact the rest of the story?

Sequencing

A1

Provide a timeline of major events in the story. Circle the three most important.

Theme/Concept

C3

What ideas are central to understanding the story? If you were to change the title, what would it be? Why do you think Lawrence chose this title?

Inference

C2

What evidence is there in the story that indicates it will end the way it does?

Literary Elements

C1

What are the qualities that Hester reveals about herself in the story?

THE ROCKING-HORSE WINNER

D3

Creative Synthesis

Create a poem or picture about one scene in the story. Why did you select the scene you did?

Summarizing

D2

Summarize the meaning of the rocking horse in the story.

Paraphrasing

D1

Paraphrase the meaning of the first paragraph of the story. How does it set the stage for what follows?

THE ROCKING-HORSE WINNER

The Gift of the Magi
by O. Henry

One dollar and eighty-seven cents. That was all. And 60 cents of it was in pennies. Pennies saved one and two at a time by bulldozing the grocer and the vegetable man and the butcher until one's cheeks burned with the silent imputation of parsimony that such close dealing implied. Three times Della counted it. One dollar and eighty-seven cents. And the next day would be Christmas.

There was clearly nothing to do but flop down on the shabby little couch and howl. So Della did it. Which instigates the moral reflection that life is made up of sobs, sniffles, and smiles, with sniffles predominating.

While the mistress of the home is gradually subsiding from the first stage to the second, take a look at the home. A furnished flat at $8 per week. It did not exactly beggar description, but it certainly had that word on the lookout for the mendicancy squad.

In the vestibule below belonged to this flat a letter-box into which no letter would go, and an electric button from which no mortal finger could coax a ring. Also appertaining thereunto was a card bearing the name "Mr. James Dillingham Young."

The "Dillingham" had been flung to the breeze during a former period of prosperity when its possessor was being paid $30 per week. Now, when the income was shrunk to $20, the letters of "Dillingham" looked blurred, as though they were thinking seriously of contracting to a modest and unassuming D. But whenever Mr. James Dillingham Young came home and reached his flat above he was called "Jim" and greatly hugged by Mrs. James Dillingham Young, already introduced to you as Della. Which is all very good.

Della finished her cry and attended to her cheeks with the powder rag. She stood by the window and looked out dully at a gray cat walking a gray fence in a gray backyard. Tomorrow would be Christmas Day, and she had only $1.87 with which to buy Jim a present. She had been saving every penny she could for months, with this result. Twenty dollars a week doesn't go far. Expenses had been greater than she had calculated. They always are. Only $1.87 to buy a present for Jim. Her Jim. Many a happy hour she had spent planning for something nice for him. Something fine and rare and sterling—something just a little bit near to being worthy of the honor of being owned by Jim.

There was a pier-glass between the windows of the room. Perhaps you have seen a pier-glass in an $8 flat. A very thin and very agile person may, by observing his reflection in a rapid sequence of longitudinal strips, obtain a fairly accurate conception of his looks. Della, being slender, had mastered the art.

Suddenly she whirled from the window and stood before the glass. Her eyes were shining brilliantly, but her face had lost its color within twenty seconds. Rapidly she pulled down her hair and let it fall to its full length.

Now, there were two possessions of the James Dillingham Youngs in which they both took a mighty pride. One was Jim's gold watch that had been his father's and his grandfather's. The other was Della's hair. Had the Queen of Sheba lived in the flat across the airshaft, Della would have let her hair hang out the window some day to dry just to depreciate Her Majesty's jewels and gifts. Had King Solomon been the janitor, with all his treasures piled up in the basement, Jim would have pulled out his watch every time he passed, just to see him pluck at his beard from envy.

So now Della's beautiful hair fell about her, rippling and shining like a cascade of brown waters. It reached below her knee and made itself almost a garment for her. And then she did it up again nervously and quickly. Once she faltered for a minute and stood still while a tear or two splashed on the worn red carpet.

On went her old brown jacket; on went her old brown hat. With a whirl of skirts and with the brilliant sparkle still in her eyes, she fluttered out the door and down the stairs to the street.

Where she stopped the sign read: "Mme. Sofronie. Hair Goods of All Kinds." One flight up Della ran, and collected herself, panting, before Madame, large, too white, chilly and hardly looking the "Sofronie."

"Will you buy my hair?" asked Della.

"I buy hair," said Madame. "Take yer hat off and let's have a sight at the looks of it."

Down rippled the brown cascade.

"Twenty dollars," said Madame, lifting the mass with a practised hand.

"Give it to me quick," said Della.

Oh, and the next two hours tripped by on rosy wings. Forget the hashed metaphor. She was ransacking the stores for Jim's present.

She found it at last. It surely had been made for Jim and no one else. There was none other like it in any of the stores, and she had turned all of them inside out. It was a platinum fob chain simple and chaste in design, properly proclaiming its value by substance alone and not by meretricious ornamentation—as all good things should do. It was even worthy of The Watch. As soon as she saw it she knew that it must be Jim's. It was like him. Quietness and value—the description applied to both. Twenty-one dollars they took from her for it, and she hurried home with the 87 cents. With that chain on his watch Jim might be properly anxious about the time in any company. Grand as the watch was, he sometimes looked at it on the sly on account of the old leather strap that he used in place of a chain.

When Della reached home her intoxication gave way a little to prudence and reason. She got out her curling irons and lighted the gas and went to work repairing the ravages made by generosity added to love. Which is always a tremendous task, dear friends—a mammoth task.

Within forty minutes her head was covered with tiny, close-lying curls that made her look wonderfully like a truant schoolboy. She looked at her reflection in the mirror long, carefully, and critically.

"If Jim doesn't kill me," she said to herself, "before he takes a second look at me, he'll say I look like a Coney Island chorus girl. But what could I do—oh, what could I do with a dollar and eighty-seven cents?"

At 7 o'clock the coffee was made and the frying pan was on the back of the stove hot and ready to cook the chops.

Jim was never late. Della doubled the fob chain in her hand and sat on the corner of the table near the door that he always entered. Then she heard his step on the stair away down on the first flight, and she turned white for just a moment. She had a habit of saying little silent prayers about the simplest everyday things, and now she whispered: "Please God, make him think I am still pretty."

The door opened and Jim stepped in and closed it. He looked thin and very serious. Poor fellow, he was only twenty-two—and to be burdened with a family! He needed a new overcoat and he was without gloves.

Jim stopped inside the door, as immovable as a setter at the scent of quail. His eyes were fixed upon Della, and there was an expression in them that she could not read, and it terrified her. It was not anger, nor surprise, nor disapproval, nor horror, nor any of the sentiments that she had been prepared for. He simply stared at her fixedly with that peculiar expression on his face.

Della wriggled off the table and went for him.

"Jim, darling," she cried, "don't look at me that way. I had my hair cut off and sold it because I couldn't have lived through Christmas without giving you a present. It'll grow again—you won't mind, will you? I just had to do it. My hair grows awfully fast. Say 'Merry Christmas!' Jim, and let's be happy. You don't know what a nice—what a beautiful, nice gift I've got for you."

"You've cut off your hair?" asked Jim, laboriously, as if he had not arrived at that patent fact yet even after the hardest mental labor.

"Cut it off and sold it," said Della. "Don't you like me just as well, anyhow? I'm me without my hair, ain't I?"

Jim looked about the room curiously.

"You say your hair is gone?" he said, with an air almost of idiocy.

"You needn't look for it," said Della. "It's sold, I tell you—sold and gone, too. It's Christmas Eve, boy. Be good to me, for it went for you. Maybe the hairs of my head were numbered," she went on with sudden serious sweetness, "but nobody could ever count my love for you. Shall I put the chops on, Jim?"

Out of his trance Jim seemed to quickly wake. He enfolded his Della. For ten seconds let us regard with discreet scrutiny some inconsequential object in the other direction. Eight dollars a week or a million a year—what is the difference? A mathematician or a wit would give you the wrong answer. The magi brought valuable gifts, but that was not among them. This dark assertion will be illuminated later on.

Jim drew a package from his overcoat pocket and threw it upon the table.

"Don't make any mistake, Dell," he said, "about me. I don't think there's anything in the way of a haircut or a shave or a shampoo that could make me like my girl any less. But if you'll unwrap that package you may see why you had me going awhile at first."

White fingers and nimble tore at the string and paper. And then an ecstatic scream of joy; and then, alas! a quick feminine change to hysterical tears and wails, necessitating the immediate employment of all the comforting powers of the lord of the flat.

For there lay The Combs—the set of combs, side and back, that Della had worshipped for long in a Broadway window. Beautiful combs, pure tortoise shell, with jeweled rims—just the shade to wear in the beautiful vanished hair. They were expensive combs, she knew, and her heart had simply craved and yearned over them without the least hope of possession. And now, they were hers, but the tresses that should have adorned the coveted adornments were gone.

But she hugged them to her bosom, and at length she was able to look up with dim eyes and a smile and say: "My hair grows so fast, Jim!"

And then Della leaped up like a little singed cat and cried, "Oh, oh!"

Jim had not yet seen his beautiful present. She held it out to him eagerly upon her open palm. The dull, precious metal seemed to flash with a reflection of her bright and ardent spirit.

"Isn't it a dandy, Jim? I hunted all over town to find it. You'll have to look at the time a hundred times a day now. Give me your watch. I want to see how it looks on it."

Instead of obeying, Jim tumbled down on the couch and put his hands under the back of his head and smiled.

"Dell," said he, "let's put our Christmas presents away and keep 'em a while. They're too nice to use just at present. I sold the watch to get the money to buy your combs. And now suppose you put the chops on."

The magi, as you know, were wise men—wonderfully wise men—who brought gifts to the Babe in the manger. They invented the art of giving Christmas gifts. Being wise, their gifts were no doubt wise ones, possibly bearing the privilege of exchange in case of duplication. And here I have lamely related to you the uneventful chronicle of two foolish children in a flat who most unwisely sacrificed for each other the greatest treasures of their house. But in a last word to the wise of these days let it be said that of all who give gifts these two were the wisest. Of all who give and receive gifts, such as they are wisest. Everywhere they are wisest. They are the magi.

Theme/Concept

C3

The concept of love is explored in the story through the action of its characters. How is this theme used to show irony in the story?

Inference

C2

What evidence does O. Henry present early in the story to show that the couple love each other?

Literary Elements

C1

What qualities of character do the couple each possess?

THE GIFT OF THE MAGI

Creative Synthesis

D3

Create a short essay describing a situation where you gave up your most precious possession for someone else.

Summarizing

D2

Summarize the story.

Paraphrasing

D1

Paraphrase what O. Henry means when he says Jim and Della are magi.

THE GIFT OF THE MAGI

THE GIFT OF THE MAGI

Using Emotion

E3

How did you react to the short story? How did it make you feel? How does O. Henry accomplish that?

Expressing Emotion

E2

Express the emotions described in the story in a poem or cartoon.

Understanding Emotion

E1

This story may be interpreted as an illustration of how acting on emotion may not yield the best results. What is your interpretation of the actions of Della and her husband?

The Nightingale and The Rose
by Oscar Wilde

"She said that she would dance with me if I brought her red roses," cried the young Student; "but in all my garden there is no red rose."

From her nest in the holm-oak tree the Nightingale heard him, and she looked out through the leaves, and wondered.

"No red rose in all my garden!" he cried, and his beautiful eyes filled with tears. "Ah, on what little things does happiness depend! I have read all that the wise men have written, and all the secrets of philosophy are mine, yet for want of a red rose is my life made wretched."

"Here at last is a true lover," said the Nightingale. "Night after night have I sung of him, though I knew him not: night after night have I told his story to the stars, and now I see him. His hair is dark as the hyacinth-blossom, and his lips are red as the rose of his desire; but passion has made his face like pale ivory, and sorrow has set her seal upon his brow."

"The Prince gives a ball to-morrow night," murmured the young Student, "and my love will be of the company. If I bring her a red rose she will dance with me till dawn. If I bring her a red rose, I shall hold her in my arms, and she will lean her head upon my shoulder, and her hand will be clasped in mine. But there is no red rose in my garden, so I shall sit lonely, and she will pass me by. She will have no heed of me, and my heart will break."

"Here indeed is the true lover," said the Nightingale. "What I sing of, he suffers—what is joy to me, to him is pain. Surely Love is a wonderful thing. It is more precious than emeralds, and dearer than fine opals. Pearls and pomegranates cannot buy it, nor is it set forth in the marketplace. It may not be purchased of the merchants, nor can it be weighed out in the balance for gold."

"The musicians will sit in their gallery," said the young Student, "and play upon their stringed instruments, and my love will dance to the sound of the harp and the violin. She will dance so lightly that her feet will not touch the floor, and the courtiers in their gay dresses will throng round her. But with me she will not dance, for I have no red rose to give her"; and he flung himself down on the grass, and buried his face in his hands, and wept.

"Why is he weeping?" asked a little Green Lizard, as he ran past him with his tail in the air.

"Why, indeed?" said a Butterfly, who was fluttering about after a sunbeam.

"Why, indeed?" whispered a Daisy to his neighbour, in a soft, low voice.

"He is weeping for a red rose," said the Nightingale.

"For a red rose?" they cried; "how very ridiculous!" and the little Lizard, who was something of a cynic, laughed outright.

But the Nightingale understood the secret of the Student's sorrow, and she sat silent in the oak-tree, and thought about the mystery of Love.

Suddenly she spread her brown wings for flight, and soared into the air. She passed through the grove like a shadow, and like a shadow she sailed across the garden.

In the centre of the grass-plot was standing a beautiful Rose-tree, and when she saw it she flew over to it, and lit upon a spray.

"Give me a red rose," she cried, "and I will sing you my sweetest song." But the Tree shook its head.

"My roses are white," it answered; "as white as the foam of the sea, and whiter than the snow upon the mountain. But go to my brother who grows round the old sun-dial, and perhaps he will give you what you want."

So the Nightingale flew over to the Rose-tree that was growing round the old sun-dial.

"Give me a red rose," she cried, "and I will sing you my sweetest song." But the Tree shook its head.

"My roses are yellow," it answered; "as yellow as the hair of the mermaiden who sits upon an amber throne, and yellower than the daffodil that blooms in the meadow before the mower comes with his scythe. But go to my brother who grows beneath the Student's window, and perhaps he will give you what you want."

So the Nightingale flew over to the Rose-tree that was growing beneath the Student's window.

"Give me a red rose," she cried, "and I will sing you my sweetest song." But the Tree shook its head.

"My roses are red," it answered, "as red as the feet of the dove, and redder than the great fans of coral that wave and wave in the ocean-cavern. But the winter has chilled my veins, and the frost has nipped my buds, and the storm has broken my branches, and I shall have no roses at all this year."

"One red rose is all I want," cried the Nightingale, "only one red rose! Is there no way by which I can get it?"

"There is a way," answered the Tree; "but it is so terrible that I dare not tell it to you."

"Tell it to me," said the Nightingale, "I am not afraid."

"If you want a red rose," said the Tree, "you must build it out of music by moonlight, and stain it with your own heart's-blood. You must sing to me with your breast against a thorn. All night long you must sing to me, and the thorn must pierce your heart, and your life-blood must flow into my veins, and become mine."

"Death is a great price to pay for a red rose," cried the Nightingale, "and Life is very dear to all. It is pleasant to sit in the green wood, and to watch the Sun in his chariot of gold, and the Moon in her chariot of pearl. Sweet is the scent of the hawthorn, and sweet are the bluebells that hide in the valley, and the heather that blows on the hill. Yet Love is better than Life, and what is the heart of a bird compared to the heart of a man?"

So she spread her brown wings for flight, and soared into the air. She swept over the garden like a shadow, and like a shadow she sailed through the grove.

The young Student was still lying on the grass, where she had left him, and the tears were not yet dry in his beautiful eyes.

"Be happy," cried the Nightingale, "be happy; you shall have your red rose. I will build it out of music by moonlight, and stain it with my own heart's-blood. All that I ask of you in return is that you will be a true lover, for Love is wiser than Philosophy, though she is wise, and mightier than Power, though he is mighty. Flame-coloured are his wings, and coloured like flame is his body. His lips are sweet as honey, and his breath is like frankincense."

The Student looked up from the grass, and listened, but he could not understand what the Nightingale was saying to him, for he only knew the things that are written down in books.

But the Oak-tree understood, and felt sad, for he was very fond of the little Nightingale who had built her nest in his branches.

"Sing me one last song," he whispered; "I shall feel very lonely when you are gone."

So the Nightingale sang to the Oak-tree, and her voice was like water bubbling from a silver jar.

When she had finished her song the Student got up, and pulled a note-book and a lead-pencil out of his pocket.

"She has form," he said to himself, as he walked away through the grove—"that cannot be denied to her; but has she got feeling? I am afraid not. In fact, she is like most artists; she is all style, without any sincerity. She would not sacrifice herself for others. She thinks merely of music, and everybody knows that the arts are selfish. Still, it must be admitted that she has some beautiful notes in her voice. What a pity it is that they do not mean anything, or do any practical good." And he went into his room, and lay down on his little pallet-bed, and began to think of his love; and, after a time, he fell asleep.

And when the Moon shone in the heavens the Nightingale flew to the Rose-tree, and set her breast against the thorn. All night long she sang with her breast against the thorn, and the cold crystal Moon leaned down and listened. All night long she sang, and the thorn went deeper and deeper into her breast, and her life-blood ebbed away from her.

She sang first of the birth of love in the heart of a boy and a girl. And on the top-most spray of the Rose-tree there blossomed a marvellous rose, petal following petal, as song followed song. Pale was it, at first, as the mist that hangs over the river—pale as the feet of the morning, and silver as the wings of the dawn. As the shadow of a rose in a mirror of silver, as the shadow of a rose in a water-pool, so was the rose that blossomed on the topmost spray of the Tree.

But the Tree cried to the Nightingale to press closer against the thorn. "Press closer, little Nightingale," cried the Tree, "or the Day will come before the rose is finished."

So the Nightingale pressed closer against the thorn, and louder and louder grew her song, for she sang of the birth of passion in the soul of a man and a maid.

And a delicate flush of pink came into the leaves of the rose, like the flush in the face of the bridegroom when he kisses the lips of the bride. But the thorn had not yet reached her heart, so the rose's heart remained white, for only a Nightingale's heart's-blood can crimson the heart of a rose.

And the Tree cried to the Nightingale to press closer against the thorn. "Press closer, little Nightingale," cried the Tree, "or the Day will come before the rose is finished."

So the Nightingale pressed closer against the thorn, and the thorn touched her heart, and a fierce pang of pain shot through her. Bitter, bitter was the pain, and wilder and wilder grew her song, for she sang of the Love that is perfected by Death, of the Love that dies not in the tomb.

And the marvellous rose became crimson, like the rose of the eastern sky. Crimson was the girdle of petals, and crimson as a ruby was the heart.

But the Nightingale's voice grew fainter, and her little wings began to beat, and a film came over her eyes. Fainter and fainter grew her song, and she felt something choking her in her throat.

Then she gave one last burst of music. The white Moon heard it, and she forgot the dawn, and lingered on in the sky. The red rose heard it, and it trembled all over with ecstasy, and opened its petals to the cold morning air. Echo bore it to her purple cavern in the hills, and woke the sleeping shepherds from their dreams. It floated through the reeds of the river, and they carried its message to the sea.

"Look, look!" cried the Tree, "the rose is finished now"; but the Nightingale made no answer, for she was lying dead in the long grass, with the thorn in her heart.

And at noon the Student opened his window and looked out.

"Why, what a wonderful piece of luck!" he cried; "here is a red rose! I have never seen any rose like it in all my life. It is so beautiful that I am sure it has a long Latin name"; and he leaned down and plucked it.

Then he put on his hat, and ran up to the Professor's house with the rose in his hand.

The daughter of the Professor was sitting in the doorway winding blue silk on a reel, and her little dog was lying at her feet.

"You said that you would dance with me if I brought you a red rose," cried the Student. "Here is the reddest rose in all the world. You will wear it to-night next your heart, and as we dance together it will tell you how I love you."

But the girl frowned.

"I am afraid it will not go with my dress," she answered; "and, besides, the Chamberlain's nephew has sent me some real jewels, and everybody knows that jewels cost far more than flowers."

"Well, upon my word, you are very ungrateful," said the Student angrily; and he threw the rose into the street, where it fell into the gutter, and a cart-wheel went over it.

"Ungrateful!" said the girl. "I tell you what, you are very rude; and, after all, who are you? Only a Student. Why, I don't believe you have even got silver buckles to your shoes as the Chamberlain's nephew has"; and she got up from her chair and went into the house.

"What I a silly thing Love is," said the Student as he walked away. "It is not half as useful as Logic, for it does not prove anything, and it is always telling one of things that are not going to happen, and making one believe things that are not true. In fact, it is quite unpractical, and, as in this age to be practical is everything, I shall go back to Philosophy and study Metaphysics."

So he returned to his room and pulled out a great dusty book, and began to read.

Consequences and Implications

A3

What are the implications of trying to win the affections of the opposite sex from this story?

Cause and Effect

A2

What causes the young man to be rejected? What does it reveal about the young woman's character?

Sequencing

A1

What are the major sections of the story? List them and describe the major events in each.

THE NIGHTINGALE AND THE ROSE

Theme/Concept

C3

The nightingale gives new meaning to the notion of sacrifice.
How does this concept work throughout the story?

Inference

C2

What evidence do we have that the nightingale will not survive?

Literary Elements

C1

What qualities emerge in each of the central characters: the
young man, the young woman, and the nightingale?

THE NIGHTINGALE AND THE ROSE

Using Emotion

E3

Who do you identify with in this story and why?

Expressing Emotion

E2

Express your feeling for the nightingale in a short poem.

Understanding Emotion

E1

How does Wilde help us see two versions of love in the story? What are those versions, seen from the perspective of the nightingale and the young woman?

THE NIGHTINGALE AND THE ROSE

The Tell-Tale Heart

by Edgar Allen Poe

TRUE!—nervous—very, very dreadfully nervous I had been and am; but why *will* you say that I am mad? The disease had sharpened my senses—not destroyed—not dulled them. Above all was the sense of hearing acute. I heard all things in the heaven and in the earth. I heard many things in hell. How, then, am I mad? Hearken! and observe how healthily—how calmly I can tell you the whole story.

It is impossible to say how first the idea entered my brain; but once conceived, it haunted me day and night. Object there was none. Passion there was none. I loved the old man. He had never wronged me. He had never given me insult. For his gold I had no desire. I think it was his eye! yes, it was this! He had the eye of a vulture—a pale blue eye, with a film over it. Whenever it fell upon me, my blood ran cold; and so by degrees—very gradually—I made up my mind to take the life of the old man, and thus rid myself of the eye forever.

Now this is the point. You fancy me mad. Madmen know nothing. But you should have seen *me*. You should have seen how wisely I proceeded—with what caution—with what foresight—with what dissimulation I went to work! I was never kinder to the old man than during the whole week before I killed him. And every night, about midnight, I turned the latch of his door and opened it—oh so gently! And then, when I had made an opening sufficient for my head, I put in a dark lantern, all closed, closed, that no light shone out, and then I thrust in my head. Oh, you would have laughed to see how cunningly I thrust it in! I moved it slowly—very, very slowly, so that I might not disturb the old man's sleep. It took me an hour to place my whole head within the opening so far that I could see him as he lay upon his bed. Ha! would a madman have been so wise as this? And then, when my head was well in the room, I undid the lantern cautiously—oh, so cautiously—cautiously (for the hinges creaked)—I undid it just so much that a single thin ray fell upon the vulture eye. And this I did for seven long nights—every night just at midnight—but I found the eye always closed; and so it was impossible to do the work; for it was not the old man who vexed me, but his Evil Eye. And every morning, when the day broke, I went boldly into the chamber, and spoke courageously to him, calling him by name in a hearty tone, and inquiring how he has passed the night. So you see he would have been a very profound old man, indeed, to suspect that every night, just at twelve, I looked in upon him while he slept.

Upon the eighth night I was more than usually cautious in opening the door. A watch's minute hand moves more quickly than did mine. Never before that night had I felt the extent of my own powers—of my sagacity. I could scarcely contain my feelings of triumph. To think that there I was, opening the door, little by little, and he not even to dream of my secret deeds or thoughts. I fairly chuckled at the idea; and perhaps he heard me; for he moved on the bed suddenly, as if startled. Now you may think that I drew back—but no. His room was as black as pitch with the thick darkness (for the shutters were close fastened, through fear of robbers), and so I knew that he could not see the opening of the door, and I kept pushing it on steadily, steadily.

I had my head in, and was about to open the lantern, when my thumb slipped upon the tin fastening, and the old man sprang up in bed, crying out—"Who's there?"

I kept quite still and said nothing. For a whole hour I did not move a muscle, and in the meantime I did not hear him lie down. He was still sitting up in the bed listening;—just as I have done, night after night, hearkening to the death watches in the wall.

Presently I heard a slight groan, and I knew it was the groan of mortal terror. It was not a groan of pain or of grief—oh, no!—it was the low stifled sound that arises from the bottom of the soul when overcharged with awe. I knew the sound well. Many a night, just at midnight, when all the world slept, it has welled up from my own bosom, deepening, with its dreadful echo, the terrors that distracted me. I say I knew it well. I knew what the old man felt, and pitied him, although I chuckled at heart. I knew that he had been lying awake ever since the first slight noise, when he had turned in the bed. His fears had been ever since growing upon him. He had been trying to fancy them causeless, but could not. He had been saying to himself—"It is nothing but the wind in the chimney—it is only a mouse crossing the floor," or "It is merely a cricket which has made a single chirp." Yes, he had been trying to comfort himself with these suppositions: but he had found all in vain. *All in vain*; because Death, in approaching him had stalked with his black shadow before him, and enveloped the victim. And it was the mournful influence of the unperceived shadow that caused him to feel—although he neither saw nor heard—to *feel* the presence of my head within the room.

When I had waited a long time, very patiently, without hearing him lie down, I resolved to open a little—a very, very little crevice in the lantern. So I opened it—you cannot imagine how stealthily, stealthily—until, at length a simple dim ray, like the thread of the spider, shot from out the crevice and fell full upon the vulture eye.

It was open—wide, wide open—and I grew furious as I gazed upon it. I saw it with perfect distinctness—all a dull blue, with a hideous veil over it that chilled the very marrow in my bones; but I could see nothing else of the old man's face or person: for I had directed the ray as if by instinct, precisely upon the damned spot.

And have I not told you that what you mistake for madness is but overacuteness of the sense?—now, I say, there came to my ears a low, dull, quick sound, such as a watch makes when enveloped in cotton. I knew that sound well, too. It was the beating of the old man's heart. It increased my fury, as the beating of a drum stimulates the soldier into courage.

But even yet I refrained and kept still. I scarcely breathed. I held the lantern motionless. I tried how steadily I could maintain the ray upon the eye. Meantime the hellish tattoo of the heart increased. It grew quicker and quicker, and louder and louder every instant. The old man's terror *must* have been extreme! It grew louder, I say, louder every moment!—do you mark me well? I have told you that I am nervous: so I am. And now at the dead hour of the night, amid the dreadful silence of that old house, so strange a noise as this excited me to uncontrollable terror. Yet, for some minutes longer I refrained and stood still. But the beating grew louder, louder! I thought the heart must burst. And now a new anxiety seized me—the sound would be heard by a neighbour! The old man's hour had come! With a loud yell, I threw open the lantern and leaped into the room. He shrieked once—once only. In an instant I dragged him to the floor, and pulled the heavy bed over him. I then smiled gaily, to find the deed so far done. But, for many minutes, the heart beat on with a muffled sound. This, however, did not vex me; it would not be heard through the wall. At length it ceased. The old man was dead. I removed the bed and examined the corpse. Yes, he was stone, stone dead. I placed my hand upon the heart and held it there many minutes. There was no pulsation. He was stone dead. His eye would trouble me no more.

If still you think me mad, you will think so no longer when I describe the wise precautions I took for the concealment of the body. The night waned, and I worked hastily, but in silence. First of all I dismembered the corpse. I cut off the head and the arms and the legs.

I then took up three planks from the flooring of the chamber, and deposited all between the scantlings. I then replaced the boards so cleverly, so cunningly, that no human eye—not even *his*—could have detected any thing wrong. There was nothing to wash out—no stain of any kind—no blood-spot whatever. I had been too wary for that. A tub had caught all—ha! ha!

When I had made an end of these labors, it was four o'clock—still dark as midnight. As the bell sounded the hour, there came a knocking at the street door. I went down to open it with a light heart,—for what had I *now* to fear? There entered three men, who introduced themselves, with perfect suavity, as officers of the police. A shriek had been heard by a neighbour during the night; suspicion of foul play had been aroused; information had been lodged at the police office, and they (the officers) had been deputed to search the premises.

I smiled,—for *what* had I to fear? I bade the gentlemen welcome. The shriek, I said, was my own in a dream. The old man, I mentioned, was absent in the country. I took my visitors all over the house. I bade them search—search well. I led them, at length, to his chamber. I showed them his treasures, secure, undisturbed. In the enthusiasm of my confidence, I brought chairs into the room, and desired them here to rest from their fatigues, while I myself, in the wild audacity of my perfect triumph, placed my own seat upon the very spot beneath which reposed the corpse of the victim.

The officers were satisfied. My *manner* had convinced them. I was singularly at ease. They sat, and while I answered cheerily, they chatted of familiar things. But, ere long, I felt myself getting pale and wished them gone. My head ached, and I fancied a ringing in my ears: but still they sat and still chatted. The ringing became more distinct:—it continued and became more distinct: I talked more freely to get rid of the feeling: but it continued and gained definiteness—until, at length, I found that the noise was not within my ears.

No doubt I now grew *very* pale;—but I talked more fluently, and with a heightened voice. Yet the sound increased—and what could I do? It was a *low, dull, quick sound—much such a sound as a watch makes when enveloped in cotton.* I gasped for breath—and yet the officers heard it not. I talked more quickly—more vehemently; but the noise steadily increased. I arose and argued about trifles, in a high key and with violent gesticulations; but the noise steadily increased. Why *would* they not be gone? I paced the floor to and fro with heavy strides, as if excited to fury by the observations of the men—but the noise steadily increased. Oh God! what could I do? I foamed—I raved—I swore! I swung the chair upon which I had been sitting, and grated it upon the boards, but the noise arose over all and continually increased. It grew louder—louder—*louder*! And still the men chatted pleasantly, and smiled. Was it possible they heard not? Almighty God!—no, no! They heard!—they suspected!—they *knew*!—they were making a mockery of my horror!—this I thought, and this I think. But anything was better than this agony! Anything was more tolerable than this derision! I could bear those hypocritical smiles no longer! I felt that I must scream or die! and now—again!—hark! louder! louder! louder! *louder*!—

"Villains!" I shrieked, "dissemble no more! I admit the deed!—tear up the planks! here, here!—It is the beating of his hideous heart!"

THE TELL-TALE HEART

Theme/Concept

C3

The concept of guilt is never explicitly mentioned in the story, yet it is central to the story. Describe how Poe uses the concept of guilt.

Inference

C2

What inference can you draw from the narrator's spoken reason for the killing?

Literary Elements

C1

What qualities in the narrator suggest that he is mad?

Creative Synthesis

D3

Create a short story that depicts a character like Poe's in respect to his not being able to conceal his crime.

Summarizing

D2

Summarize the plot of the story.

Paraphrasing

D1

Paraphrase the lines that best reveal the madness of the narrator.

THE TELL-TALE HEART

Using Emotion

E3

Poe manipulates the emotions of the reader by using strong emotion in his central character. What techniques does he use to portray the narrator's emotions?

Expressing Emotion

E2

Using a similar technique to Poe, express an emotion (e.g., hate, love, envy, shame) in a short monologue.

Understanding Emotion

E1

What emotions does the narrator reveal he feels about the man? Why does he kill him?

THE TELL-TALE HEART

Ugly
by Guy de Maupassant

Certainly, at this blessed epoch of equality of mediocrity, of rectangular abomination, as Edgar Allan Poe says—at this delightful period, when everybody dreams of resembling everybody else, so that it has become impossible to tell the President of the Republic from a waiter—in these days, which are the forerunners of that promising, blissful day, when everything in this world will be of a dull, neutral uniformity, certainly at such an epoch, one has the right, or rather it is one's duty, to be ugly.

Lebeau, however, assuredly exercised that right with the most cruel vigor. He fulfilled that duty with the fiercest heroism, and to make matters worse, the mysterious irony of fate had caused him to be born with the name of Lebeau, while an ingenious godfather, the unconscious accomplice of the pranks of destiny, had given him the Christian name of Antinous.

Even among our contemporaries, who were already on the highroad to the coming ideal of universal hideousness, Antinous Lebeau was remarkable for his ugliness; and one might have said that he positively threw zeal, too much zeal, into the matter, though he was not hideous like Mirabeau, who made the people exclaim: "Oh! the beautiful monster!"

Alas! No. He was without any beauty of ugliness. He was ugly, that was all; nothing more nor less; in short, he was uglily ugly. He was not humpbacked, nor knock-kneed, nor pot-bellied; his legs were not like a pair of tongs, and his arms were neither too long nor too short, and yet, there was an utter lack of uniformity about him, not only in painters' eyes, but also in everybody's, for nobody could meet him in the street without turning to look after him, and thinking: "Good heavens! What an object."

His hair was of no particular color; a light chestnut, mixed with yellow. There was not much of it; but still, he was not absolutely bald, but just bald enough to allow his butter-colored pate to show. Butter-colored? Hardly! The color of margarine would be more applicable, and such pale margarine!

His face was also like margarine, but of adulterated margarine, certainly. His cranium, the color of unadulterated margarine, looked almost like butter in comparison.

There was very little to say about his mouth! Less than little; the sum total was—nothing. It was a chimerical mouth.

But take it that I have said nothing about him, and let us replace this vain description by the useful formula: "Impossible to describe." But you must not forget that Antinous Lebeau was ugly, that the fact impressed everybody as soon as they saw him, and that nobody remembered ever having seen an uglier person; and let us add, as the climax of his misfortune, that he thought so himself.

From this you will see that he was not a fool, and not ill-natured, either; but, of course, he was unhappy. An unhappy man thinks only of his wretchedness, and people take his nightcap for a fool's cap; while, on the other hand, goodness is only esteemed when it is cheerful. Consequently, Antinous Lebeau passed for a fool, and an ill-tempered fool; he was not even pitied because he was so ugly!

He had only one pleasure in life, and that was to go and roam about the darkest streets on dark nights, and to hear the street-walkers say:

"Come home with me, you handsome, dark man!"

It was, alas! a furtive pleasure, and he knew that it was not true. For, occasionally, when the woman was old or drunk and he profited by the invitation, as soon as the candle was lighted in the garret, they no longer murmured the fallacious "handsome, dark man." When they saw him, the old women grew still older, and the drunken women got sober. And more than one, although hardened against disgust, and ready for all risks, said to him, and in spite of his liberal payment:

"My little man, I must say you are most confoundedly ugly."

At last, however, he renounced even that lamentable pleasure, when he heard the still more lamentable words which a wretched woman could not help uttering when he went home with her:

"Well, I must have been very hungry!"

Alas! It was he who was a hungry, unhappy man; hungry for something that should resemble love, were it ever so little; he longed not to live like a pariah any more, not to be exiled and proscribed by his ugliness. And the ugliest, the most repugnant woman would have appeared beautiful to him, if she would only not think him ugly, or, at any rate, not tell him so, and not let him see that she felt horror at him on that account.

The consequence was, that, when he one day met a poor, blear-eyed creature, with her face covered with scabs, and bearing evident signs of alcoholism, with a driveling mouth, and ragged and filthy petticoats, to whom he gave liberal alms, for which she kissed his hand, he took her home with him, had her cleansed, dressed and taken care of, made her his servant, and then his housekeeper. Next he raised her to the rank of his mistress, and, finally, of course, he married her.

She was almost as ugly as he was! Almost, but certainly not quite; for she was hideous, and her hideousness had its charm and its beauty, no doubt; that something by which a woman can attract a man. And she had proved that by deceiving him, and she let him see it better still, by seducing another man.

That other man was actually uglier than he was.

He was certainly uglier, a collection of every physical and moral ugliness, a companion of beggars whom she had picked up among her former vagrant associates, a jailbird, a dealer in little girls, a vagabond covered with filth, with legs like a toad's, with a mouth like a lamprey's, and a death's-head, in which the nose had been replaced by two holes.

"And you have wronged me with a wretch like that," the poor cuckold said. "And in my own house! And in such a manner that I might catch you in the very act! And why, why, you wretch? Why, seeing that he is uglier than I am?"

"Oh no!" she exclaimed. "You may say what you like, that I am a dirty slut and a strumpet, but do not say that he is uglier than you are."

And the unhappy man stood there, vanquished and overcome by her last words, which she uttered without understanding all the horror which he would feel at them.

"Because, you see, he has his own particular ugliness, while you are merely ugly like everybody else is."

Generalizations

B3

What generalization or moral can be made from this story?

Classifications

UGLY

B2

What are the different classifications of "ugly" suggested in the story?

Details

B1

List the examples of ugliness that are given.

Creative Synthesis

D3

Create a story about a concept you are interested in that uses this story as a model. The concept may be beauty, strength, courage, or justice, or you may select your own.

Summarizing

D2

Summarize the meaning of the story for a young child. How have you adapted your summary based on the age of the audience?

Paraphrasing

D1

Paraphrase the last line of the story.

UGLY

Name: _____ Date: _____

Using Emotion

E3

The concept of appearance is central to our understanding of our own identity, as it reflects how others see us and how we present ourselves to the world. What emotions do we associate with being perceived as ugly? With seeing ourselves as ugly?

Expressing Emotion

E2

Can you remember a time when you might have been called ugly (or stupid)? How did it make you feel? Write a short essay describing that situation.

Understanding Emotion

E1

How does de Maupassant use humor to convey his ideas about being ugly?

UGLY

A Haunted House

by Virginia Woolf

Whatever hour you woke there was a door shutting. From room to room they went, hand in hand, lifting here, opening there, making sure—a ghostly couple.

"Here we left it," she said. And he added, "Oh, but here too!" "It's upstairs," she murmured. "And in the garden," he whispered. "Quietly," they said, "or we shall wake them."

But it wasn't that you woke us. Oh, no. "They're looking for it; they're drawing the curtain," one might say, and so read on a page or two. "Now they've found it," one would be certain, stopping the pencil on the margin. And then, tired of reading, one might rise and see for oneself, the house all empty, the doors standing open, only the wood pigeons bubbling with content and the hum of the threshing machine sounding from the farm. "What did I come in here for? What did I want to find?" My hands were empty. "Perhaps it's upstairs then?" The apples were in the loft. And so

down again, the garden still as ever, only the book had slipped into the grass.

But they had found it in the drawing room. Not that one could ever see them. The windowpanes reflected apples, reflected roses; all the leaves were green in the glass. If they moved in the drawing room, the apple only turned its yellow side. Yet, the moment after, if the door was opened, spread about the floor, hung upon the walls, pendant from the ceiling—what? My hands were empty. The shadow of a thrush crossed the carpet; from the deepest wells of silence the wood pigeon drew its bubble of sound. "Safe, safe, safe," the pulse of the house beat softly. "The treasure buried; the room . . ." the pulse stopped short. Oh, was that the buried treasure?

A moment later the light had faded. Out in the garden then? But the trees spun darkness for a wandering beam of sun. So fine, so rare, coolly sunk beneath the surface the beam I sought always burned behind the glass. Death was the glass; death was between us, coming to the woman first, hundreds of years ago, leaving the house, sealing all the windows; the rooms were darkened. He left it, left her, went North, went East, saw the stars turned in the Southern sky; sought the house, found it dropped beneath the Downs. "Safe, safe, safe," the pulse of the house beat gladly. "The Treasure yours."

The wind roars up the avenue. Trees stoop and bend this way and that. Moonbeams splash and spill wildly in the rain. But the beam of the lamp falls straight from the window. The candle burns stiff and still. Wandering through the house, opening the windows, whispering not to wake us, the ghostly couple seek their joy.

"Here we slept," she says. And he adds, "Kisses without number." "Waking in the morning—" "Silver between the trees—" "Upstairs—" "In the garden—" "When summer came—" "In winter snowtime—" The doors go shutting far in the distance, gently knocking like the pulse of a heart.

Nearer they come, cease at the doorway. The wind falls, the rain slides silver down the glass. Our eyes darken, we hear no steps beside us; we see no lady spread her ghostly cloak. His hands shield the lantern. "Look," he breathes. "Sound asleep. Love upon their lips."

Stooping, holding their silver lamp above us, long they look and deeply. Long they pause. The wind drives straightly; the flame stoops slightly. Wild beams of moonlight cross both floor and wall, and, meeting, stain the faces bent; the faces pondering; the faces that search the sleepers and seek their hidden joy.

"Safe, safe, safe," the heart of the house beats proudly. "Long years—" he sighs. "Again you found me." "Here," she murmurs, "sleeping; in the garden reading; laughing, rolling apples in the loft. Here we left our treasure—" Stooping, their light lifts the lids upon my eyes. "Safe! safe! safe!" the pulse of the house beats wildly. Waking, I cry "Oh, is this your buried treasure? The light in the heart."

Consequences and Implications

A3

What are the implications for the new owner of having experienced the presence of the ghost couple?

Cause and Effect

A2

What caused the ghosts to return?

Sequencing

A1

What is the order of the events that the ghosts act out? What is the significance of the book? Of the garden?

A HAUNTED HOUSE

Theme/Concept

C3

What might be another title for the story? Why?

Inference

C2

What evidence in the story suggests that they loved each other?

Literary Elements

C1

What qualities do the ghost couple reveal about themselves?

A HAUNTED HOUSE

Creative Synthesis

D3

Create a poem or visual that uses a ghost as a central character or force in the depiction of lost love returned.

Summarizing

D2

Summarize the nature of the haunting.

Paraphrasing

D1

Paraphrase the last statement of the current occupant of the house.

A HAUNTED HOUSE

CHAPTER
2

Poetry

Chapter 2 focuses on selections of classical poetry, both British and American, with corresponding ladders that fit the selection chosen. Each reading is followed by three sets of questions; each set is aligned to one of the six sets of ladder skills.

The poetry selections with their corresponding ladders are:

Name: _____   Date: _____

Ozymandias
by Percy Bysshe Shelley

I met a traveller from an antique land
Who said: Two vast and trunkless legs of stone
Stand in the desert. Near them, on the sand,
Half sunk, a shattered visage lies, whose frown,
And wrinkled lip, and sneer of cold command,
Tell that its sculptor well those passions read
Which yet survive, stamped on these lifeless things,
The hand that mocked them, and the heart that fed:
And on the pedestal these words appear:
"My name is Ozymandias, king of kings:
Look on my works, ye Mighty, and despair!"
Nothing beside remains. Round the decay
Of that colossal wreck, boundless and bare
The lone and level sands stretch far away.

Consequences and Implications

A3

What is the role of nature in this poem? What are the consequences of nature uncontrolled on manmade works?

Cause and Effect

A2

What would cause Ozymandias to construct a statue of himself? What effect does it have today? (The remains of the statue are near Luxor in Egypt.)

Sequencing

A1

What can you determine about Ozymandias from the objects left on the ground? How would you put them together? What story do they tell?

OZYMANDIAS

Theme/Concept

C3

What does this poem reveal about the concept of time? About human accomplishment?

Inference

C2

How do you think Ozymandias felt about the inscription on the pedestal? Why is this significant to the poem?

Literary Elements

C1

What are the most important words in the poem? Why?

OZYMANDIAS

Creative Synthesis

D3

Create a poem about the loss of understanding and knowledge about a past civilization due to natural or manmade disasters.

Summarizing

D2

Summarize the meaning of the poem.

Paraphrasing

D1

Rewrite the last three lines of the poem in your own words.

OZYMANDIAS

The World Is Too Much With Us

by William Wordsworth

The world is too much with us; late and soon,
Getting and spending, we lay waste our powers:
Little we see in Nature that is ours;
We have given our hearts away, a sordid boon!
This Sea that bares her bosom to the moon;
The winds that will be howling at all hours,
And are up-gathered now like sleeping flowers;
For this, for everything, we are out of tune,
It moves us not.—Great God! I'd rather be
A Pagan suckled in a creed outworn;
So might I, standing on this pleasant lea,
Have glimpses that would make me less forlorn;
Have sight of Proteus rising from the sea;
Or hear old Triton blow his wreathed horn.

..

Theme/Concept

C3

How does Wordsworth use the concept of nature to express his ideas in the poem?

Inference

C2

What inference does Wordsworth make about what is wrong with the world today? Why would he prefer to be a pagan?

Literary Elements

C1

How does Wordsworth characterize people in the world?

THE WORLD IS TOO MUCH WITH US

Creative Synthesis

D3

Create a poem in the 14-line abab rhyme scheme and style of Wordsworth to voice a similar theme.

Summarizing

D2

Summarize the meaning of the following line: "We have given our hearts away, a sordid boon!" (Sordid means dirty or tainted, and a boon is a benefit.)

Paraphrasing

D1

Paraphrase the last section of the poem, beginning with "Great God!"

THE WORLD IS TOO MUCH WITH US

Using Emotion

E3

Wordsworth wrote many poems that expressed his love of nature. How did he convey his strong feelings for the subject in this poem? Think about his use of punctuation, his choice of words and images, and his ideas. Cite as many examples as you can.

Expressing Emotion

E2

In a poem or picture, express your feelings about an object in nature that you love. Explain why you react so strongly to this object.

Understanding Emotion

E1

According to Wordsworth, why do humans feel connected to the natural world? Why do you?

THE WORLD IS TOO MUCH WITH US

Ulysses

by Alfred, Lord Tennyson

It little profits that an idle king,
By this still hearth, among these barren crags,
Match'd with an aged wife, I mete and dole
Unequal laws unto a savage race,
That hoard, and sleep, and feed, and know not me.

I cannot rest from travel: I will drink
Life to the lees; all times I have enjoy'd
Greatly, have suffer'd greatly, both with those
That lov'd me, and alone; on shore, and when
Thro' scudding drifts the rainy Hyades
Vex'd the dim sea: I am become a name;
For always roaming with a hungry heart
Much have I seen and known; cities of men
And manners, climates, councils, governments,
Myself not least, but honor'd of them all;
And drunk delight of battle with my peers,
Far on the ringing plains of windy Troy,
I am a part of all that I have met;
Yet all experience is an arch wherethro'
Gleams that untravell'd world, whose margin fades
For ever and for ever when I move.
How dull it is to pause, to make an end,
To rust unburnish'd, not to shine in use!
As tho' to breathe were life. Life pil'd on life
Were all too little, and of one to me
Little remains: but every hour is sav'd
From that eternal silence, something more,
A bringer of new things; and vile it were
For some three suns to store and hoard myself,
And this gray spirit yearning in desire
To follow knowledge like a sinking star,
Beyond the utmost bound of human thought.

This is my son, mine own Telemachus,
To whom I leave the scepter and the isle—
Well-lov'd of me, discerning to fulfil
This labor, by slow prudence to make mild
A rugged people, and thro' soft degrees
Subdue them to the useful and the good.
Most blameless is he, centred in the sphere
Of common duties, decent not to fail

In offices of tenderness, and pay
Meet adoration to my household gods,
When I am gone. He works his work, I mine.

There lies the port; the vessel puffs her sail:
There gloom the dark broad seas. My mariners,
Souls that have toil'd, and wrought, and thought with me—
That ever with a frolic welcome took
The thunder and the sunshine, and oppos'd
Free hearts, free foreheads—you and I are old;
Old age hath yet his honor and his toil;
Death closes all: but something ere the end,
Some work of noble note, may yet be done,
Not unbecoming men that strove with Gods.
The lights begin to twinkle from the rocks:
The long day wanes: the slow moon climbs: the deep
Moans round with many voices. Come, my friends,
'Tis not too late to seek a newer world.
Push off, and sitting well in order smite
The sounding furrows; for my purpose holds
To sail beyond the sunset, and the baths
Of all the western stars, until I die.
It may be that the gulfs will wash us down:
It may be we shall touch the Happy Isles,
And see the great Achilles, whom we knew.
Tho' much is taken, much abides; and tho'
We are not now that strength which in old days
Moved earth and heaven; that which we are, we are;
One equal temper of heroic hearts,
Made weak by time and fate, but strong in will
To strive, to seek, to find, and not to yield.

Name: _____ Date: _____

Theme/Concept

C3

What can you say about Ulysses in respect to loyalty, duty, or love of country? Create a generalization using one of these themes.

Inference

C2

What evidence in the poem indicates that Ulysses is now an old man?

Literary Elements

C1

What are the admirable qualities of Ulysses found in the poem?

ULYSSES

D3

Creative Synthesis

Create your own story about a hero who goes on a journey, encounters problems, overcomes them, and returns home with knowledge and wisdom he didn't have before. Be sure to answer the following questions as you write your story (use it as an outline):

- What is the hero's name?
- Where does he travel and why?
- What problems does he encounter?
- How does he overcome them?
- What does he learn?

Summarizing

D2

Summarize the most important ideas in the poem.

Paraphrasing

D1

Paraphrase the last line of the poem. How is it a recipe for living life?

ULYSSES

ULYSSES

Using Emotion

E3

How does Tennyson feel about Ulysses? How do you know?

Expressing Emotion

E2

Create a statement, poem, or drawing to express
your feelings about Ulysses as a hero.

Understanding Emotion

E1

How do Ulysses' feelings affect his actions in the poem?
Describe their effect, using the lines in the poem.

Name: _____   Date: _____

The Lake Isle of Innisfree
by William Butler Yeats

I will arise and go now, and go to Innisfree,
And a small cabin build there, of clay and wattles made:
Nine bean-rows will I have there, a hive for the honeybee,
And live alone in the bee-loud glade.

And I shall have some peace there, for peace comes dropping slow,
Dropping from the veils of the morning to where the cricket sings;
There midnight's all a glimmer, and noon a purple glow,
And evening full of the linnet's wings.

I will arise and go now, for always night and day
I hear lake water lapping with low sounds by the shore;
While I stand on the roadway, or on the pavements grey,
I hear it in the deep heart's core.

Theme/Concept

C3

The notion of what is "core" is an interesting idea in this poem. How does that concept work in the poem?

Inference

C2

What evidence does Yeats provide that the lake is an object inside him as well as outside?

Literary Elements

C1

What qualities does Yeats assign to the lake? Why does he name it Innisfree?

THE LAKE ISLE OF INNISFREE

Creative Synthesis

D3

Create a story in which water saves the heroine from destruction. Be sure to describe the qualities of your heroine, why she is in need, and how water helps her.

Summarizing

D2

Summarize your feelings about the poem.

Paraphrasing

D1

Paraphrase the line: "I hear it in the deep heart's core."

THE LAKE ISLE OF INNISFREE

Using Emotion

E3

How do thoughts and feelings mingle in this poem? How do you compensate for your struggle between thoughts and emotions?

Expressing Emotion

E2

Many people today like to vacation or live near water. Express in your own words the power water has to affect your emotions and mood.

Understanding Emotion

E1

What are the characteristics of water that cause people to want to be near it? How does it make Yeats feel?

THE LAKE ISLE OF INNISFREE

In a Library
by Emily Dickinson

A precious, mouldering pleasure 't is
To meet an antique book,
In just the dress his century wore;
A privilege, I think,

His venerable hand to take,
And warming in our own,
A passage back, or two, to make
To times when he was young.

His quaint opinions to inspect,
His knowledge to unfold
On what concerns our mutual mind,
The literature of old;

What interested scholars most,
What competitions ran
When Plato was a certainty.
And Sophocles a man;

When Sappho was a living girl,
And Beatrice wore
The gown that Dante deified.
Facts, centuries before,

He traverses familiar,
As one should come to town
And tell you all your dreams were true;
He lived where dreams were sown.

His presence is enchantment,
You beg him not to go;
Old volumes shake their vellum heads
And tantalize, just so.

Consequences and Implications

A3

According to Dickinson, what are the consequences of being in a library?

Cause and Effect

A2

What is the relationship between an old book
and the author's sense of well-being?

Sequencing

A1

What names of characters and writers does Dickinson mention? Why do
you think she chooses these particular ones in the order she provides?

IN A LIBRARY

Creative Synthesis

D3

Write an essay that describes a book you have read. What was the book and why did it affect you so powerfully?

Summarizing

D2

Summarize the central idea in the poem.

IN A LIBRARY

Paraphrasing

D1

Paraphrase the lines: "Old volumes shake their vellum heads/And tantalize, just so."

Name: _____ Date: _____

Using Emotion

E3

How do your feelings about books influence what you think about them? Describe the connection.

Expressing Emotion

E2

Illustrate these feelings as a book cover. What is the name of your book?

Understanding Emotion

E1

How do old books make you feel? Why?

IN A LIBRARY

Fire and Ice
by Robert Frost

Some say the world will end in fire,
Some say in ice.
From what I've tasted of desire
I hold with those who favor fire.
But if it had to perish twice,
I think I know enough of hate
To say that for destruction ice
Is also great
And would suffice.

Consequences and Implications

A3

What are the implications of extreme emotion that Frost is suggesting?

Cause and Effect

A2

What is the effect of extreme conditions like fire and ice on natural surroundings? How does Frost use these conditions to create symbolic representations?

Sequencing

A1

What details about the poem, such as words or images, are interesting to you?

FIRE AND ICE

Generalizations

B3

What concepts do fire and ice represent in the poem?

Classifications

B2

What categories do fire and ice belong to?

Details

B1

What are some other examples of extreme opposites like fire and ice?

FIRE AND ICE

Theme/Concept

C3

Create a poem of opposite elements, just as Frost has. You may want to choose among the following or select your own: good and evil, night and day, beauty and ugliness, or truth and lies.

Inference

C2

Explain Frost's opinion about whether he would choose to see the world end by fire or ice.

Literary Elements

C1

What human emotions does Frost assign to fire? To ice?

FIRE AND ICE

We Wear the Mask

by Paul Laurence Dunbar

We wear the mask that grins and lies,
It hides our cheeks and shades our eyes,—
This debt we pay to human guile;
With torn and bleeding hearts we smile,
And mouth with myriad subtleties.

Why should the world be over-wise,
In counting all our tears and sighs?
Nay, let them only see us, while
We wear the mask.

We smile, but, O great Christ, our cries
To thee from tortured souls arise.
We sing, but oh the clay is vile
Beneath our feet, and long the mile;
But let the world dream otherwise,
We wear the mask!

Consequences and Implications

A3

What is the implication of the "smile" in the poem? Why does Dunbar wear a mask?

Cause and Effect

A2

What causes Dunbar to want to order the words the way he does? What effect does it have on the reader?

Sequencing

A1

What words in each stanza explain the true feelings of Dunbar and his people? Identify them in Stanzas 1, 2, and 3.

WE WEAR THE MASK

Generalizations

B3

Another title of the poem could be "Duplicity." Why would that be an appropriate title? What would you title this poem and why?

Classifications

B2

What insults and injustices have African Americans experienced in this country? How would you classify them? Compare and contrast them to the prior list you made.

Details

B1

What wrongs have been committed against people because of prejudice? Make a list.

WE WEAR THE MASK

Creative Synthesis

D3

Create a poem or a visual that depicts some
form of man's inhumanity to others.

Summarizing

D2

Summarize the meaning of the mask.

Paraphrasing

D1

Paraphrase the line: "Why should the world be over-wise, /
In counting all our tears and sighs?"

WE WEAR THE MASK

CHAPTER

3

Biographies

This chapter of *Jacob's Ladder* focuses on the use of biography as a specialized form of nonfiction in order to enhance students' understanding of their own career development and to teach metacognitive skills in the process. This chapter contains five biography vignettes of famous women who contributed greatly to diverse fields of endeavor. All six ladders are used; however, more use of Ladders E and F is evident in this section. Once students have read and completed the ladders for the five biographies, additional analysis activities are included that encourage comparative analyses across the biographies.

The list of biographies with their ladders is found below:

Biographical Vignette......................... **Ladders Used**

Ada Lovelace, computer scientist............................A, B, C

Marie Curie, scientist ....A, C, F

Emily Dickinson, poet ....C, D, F

Harriet Tubman, social reformer ....A, E, F

Margaret Mead, anthropologist................................B, D, F

Ada Lovelace
Computer Scientist

Ada Augusta Byron was born in 1815, the only legitimate child of the Romantic poet, Lord Byron. Known as Lady Lovelace after marrying the Earl of Lovelace, she is now considered the first computer programmer. The U.S. Department of Defense commissioned a new computer language named after her in 1979, and the British Computer Society gives out the Lovelace Medal annually. There is even an Ada Lovelace Day celebrated internationally during which bloggers celebrate the achievements of women in science and technology. However, her claim to fame was not acknowledged as such during her lifetime.

Ada was born in London to Lord Byron and Lady Byron, who whisked the infant away shortly after she was born. Lady Byron was convinced that Lord Byron suffered from some terrible mental illness and was determined that her daughter should never know nor be anything like her father. She therefore decided that Ada would be tutored in math and science rather than English and literature.

At the time, it was highly unusual for a girl to be tutored at all, let alone in math and science. Ada was fortunate to have a wealthy mother with a background in math herself (she was known as the "princess of parallelograms") who could provide her with sufficient tutoring. It was clear very early in her life that Ada was proficient in math and quite adept at explaining mathematical concepts in symbolic and metaphoric language, although her mother struggled to maintain Ada's interest in the subject. Incapacitated with a debilitating illness of unknown origin in 1929, Ada was unable to walk for 3 years. It was during this time that she relented and her mathematical education flourished under several tutors.

Ada was introduced to Mary Somerville, an accomplished mathematician and scientist in her own right, at age 17. It was through this relationship that she learned of the works of Charles Babbage, an inventor and engineer. Babbage was working on plans for a new calculating engine, now known as the Analytical Engine. Babbage became her mentor and helped Ada matriculate at the University of London in 1840. The two remained close friends, exchanging correspondence and ideas to the extent that historians cannot be sure who came up with some of the key ideas that contributed to the birth of computers. It has been speculated that Ada herself suggested the use of punched cards as the medium to hold computational data and equations or "instructions" that would then be read by the Analytical Engine. Her proposal of a plan for how the engine might compute Bernoulli numbers, a complex algorithm, is now considered the first computer program.

In 1835, Ada married William King, who became the Earl of Lovelace just 3 years later, making Ada the Countess of Lovelace. As lady of the house, she oversaw three estates and mothered three children by 1839. However, even as she attended dutifully to her domestic obligations, she continued her mathematical endeavors.

Charles Babbage presented his Analytical Engine at an Italian seminar in 1841. Luigi Menabrea, an Italian engineer, published an article in French detailing Babbage's proposal, and Ada translated it into English for British publication. To Ada, however, Menabrea did not do the machine justice, so she added notes of her own to expand his article. Babbage was delighted with her additions and encouraged her to elaborate on them, which she did until her "translation" was three times as long as Menabrea's original article!

Ada's notes included the all-important Note G, which detailed her Bernoulli algorithm, as well as speculation that the Analytical Engine might some day be used not only for the composition of mathematical equations but for music and graphics as well. This foresight, a century ahead of its time, is one of the reasons why Ada is so retroactively admired in her field.

Babbage ensured that the article was published in Richard Taylor's *Scientific Memoirs* (Volume 3) in 1843, but Ada signed it only A. A. L., as high-class women at the time were not taken seriously as intellectuals. Only her close friends knew who "A. A. L." was for nearly 30 years, and it was not until 1953 that her notes on Babbage's Analytical Engine were recognized as the precursor to the modern computer and republished.

Ada was wracked with illnesses throughout her lifetime, but by 1843, her pain had become unmanageable. She became unwittingly addicted to laudanum, opium, and morphine, which likely contributed to her well-known hot-headedness and roller coaster mood swings. She gained a reputation for gambling and losing her temper.

Finally, in 1852, Ada Lovelace died of uterine cancer at the young age of 36. As requested, she was buried in the Byron tomb next to the father she never knew, who coincidentally also died at age 36.

Consequences and Implications

A3

What were the consequences of Ada being raised in a wealthy environment on her contributions to computer science? Do you think she would have been famous had she come from poverty? Why or why not?

Cause and Effect

A2

Ada's mother was worried about her daughter becoming mentally ill like her father. What effect do you think that particular fear had on Ada?

Sequencing

A1

Create a timeline of Ada Lovelace's life. What do you see as the three most important events in her life?

ADA LOVELACE

Generalizations

B3

What generalization can you make about Ada's role in the development of computer science as a field? How is she regarded today?

Classifications

B2

How would you classify Ada's contributions?

ADA LOVELACE

Details

B1

List the details that show how Ada Lovelace contributed to Babbage's work.

Theme/Concept

C3

Think about the following statement: "Men have been responsible for successful women." How does this theme relate to Ada's life?

Inference

C2

What evidence exists in Ada's biography to show that she was capable of translating Babbage's ideas and extending them?

Literary Elements

C1

What were the important features of Ada Lovelace's family background? How did they contribute to her ultimate success?

ADA LOVELACE

Marie Curie
Scientist

When Maria Sklodowska was born in 1867, Warsaw, Poland was hardly recognizable. At the time, Poland was under occupation by Austria, Russia, and Prussia, and Warsaw was under Russian control. Oppressive Russian laws prohibited proper math and science classes from being taught at the boarding schools where Maria's parents worked. Her father was a physicist, however, and both parents ensured that Maria and her brother and sisters received a well-rounded education. Maria's mother died of tuberculosis when Maria was only 11 years old, and although she was devastated, she continued to work hard with her tutors.

Maria was always at the top of her class even though she was in classes with older girls. She and her sister Bronislawa (Bronya) joined an illegal night school dubbed the "Floating University," because the location had to change constantly to avoid detection by the Russians. At the Floating University, they studied many subjects, always with a political mind toward bringing about the eventual independence of the Polish nation. Eventually, the sisters realized they needed a more formal education and made a pact: Maria would work to support Bronya's medical education in Paris, and when Bronya had amassed enough funds, she would bring Maria to Paris and support her education in turn.

With Bronya away in Paris, 16-year-old Maria began giving private tutoring lessons in Warsaw. She worked for 2 years but did not make enough money to support both Bronya's and her own dreams, so she moved to a small factory village and worked for the factory's owner as governess to his children. After 3 years at this job, and with a little help from her father, Maria was finally able to move to Paris in 1891 to begin studying at Paris-Sorbonne University. It was here that she changed her name to the French spelling, Marie.

Marie got her degree in physics in 2 years, followed by a degree in math a year later as well as a master's degree in physics. In 1894, she was working on her master's degree in mathematics in addition to a study of magnetism commissioned by the Society for the Encouragement of National Industry, and she needed laboratory facilities in which to work on it. She was introduced to Pierre Curie, who ran a lab in Paris at the School of Industrial Physics and Chemistry. Curie was already involved in studying magnetism, so it was a perfect match in more ways than one. Within the year, Marie and Pierre were married and hardly ever left their lab except to go bicycling across the French countryside.

Marie became a French citizen, but Poland was always on her mind. She applied for admittance to Krakow University but was denied—women were not yet permitted to attend. However, her fondness for Poland was not deterred. She hired Polish governesses to tutor both of her daughters in

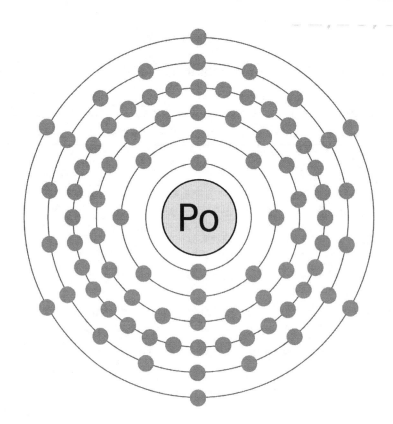

the Polish language. In 1898, when Pierre and Marie discovered a new element, they named it polonium.

In 1896, another French scientist named Henri Becquerel discovered that rays of energy similar to X-rays emitted from uranium without any outside source interacting with it. The Curies continued research on the phenomenon and called this inherent radiation "radioactivity." Marie figured out how to prove the existence of this strange energy by using a device, called the electrometer, previously invented by Pierre and his brother. By sampling the air around the uranium, she determined that it was causing the air to conduct electrical currents. The Curies and Becquerel shared the 1903 Nobel Prize in Physics for these discoveries, but it was Marie who came up with the theory of radioactivity as well as the manner for measuring it.

Around the same time, the Curies had discovered yet another new radioactive element that they named radium. However, radium could only be found in scant traces; it took one ton of ore to isolate one tenth of a gram of radium. Marie and Pierre worked tirelessly to obtain pure radium metal even after Marie came up with a more efficient way of isolating the element. Many scientists, once they create such a process, immediately patent it so that they alone can freely use it. However, Marie saw the great possibilities for radium and decided not to patent it, thus granting the global scientific community free reign over radium research. In 1911, she won the Nobel Prize in Chemistry for her work with radium and the isolation process.

Name: _____ Date: _____

Tragedy struck the pair when Pierre was hit by a horse-drawn wagon while crossing the street and died. Grief-stricken but determined to continue their work, Marie began teaching his classes and eventually took his post as professor of general physics, having earned her doctoral degree in 1903. She was the first female professor at the Sorbonne. Marie brilliantly saw the potential for radium in the medical field as radioactivity could be used for imaging machines. During World War I, she and her daughter outfitted vehicles and trained 150 nurses with X-ray technology so that medics could find bullets and shrapnel in wounded soldiers and perform emergency surgery on the battlefield without moving the patients.

Marie Curie founded and directed the Radium Institute in Paris, which was renamed the Curie Institute after her death. She also founded the Radium Institute in Warsaw, which Bronya (by then a doctor) directed; it was also renamed for her posthumously. She received two Nobel Prizes and various other scientific accolades. Her daughter, Irène Joliot-Curie, went on to win the Nobel Prize in Chemistry in 1935. Marie Curie's influence on modern physics and medicine is truly remarkable. Unfortunately, her dedication and devotion to her work led to her demise. She died of leukemia in 1934—attributed to her decades-long exposure to radioactive elements.

Consequences and Implications

A3

What were the implications of gender on Marie's accomplishments?

Cause and Effect

A2

How did the discovery of radium affect Marie's later discoveries?

Sequencing

A1

It is often said that one success leads to another. How is this illustrated in the life of Marie Curie? Sequence the series of positive events.

MARIE CURIE

Theme/Concept

C3

If you were to write an epitaph for Marie to be placed
on her tombstone, what would it be? Why?

Inference

C2

What inferences can you draw from Marie's early life in Poland
and how it influenced her later successes and failures?

Literary Elements

C1

What were Marie Curie's strongest characteristics? How
did these traits help her to be a successful scientist?

MARIE CURIE

Reflecting

F3

The role of mentors in the development of scientific talent is important for success. How did mentors help Marie?

Monitoring and Assessing

F2

Marie's accomplishments were extraordinary and highly rewarded even though most scientists do not receive that degree of recognition for their work. What might be appropriate markers to strive for in a scientific career?

Planning and Goal Setting

F1

Based on Marie's Curie's life, what advice would you give to young women who want to be successful scientists? How would your advice be different for young men?

MARIE CURIE

Emily Dickinson
Poet

Emily Dickinson is arguably the most well-known American literary voice. Her uninhibited form and witty, irreverent turns of phrase have endeared her to writers and feminists for more than a century. Although her poems were characteristically short, she explored passionate emotions like love, fear, and hope as well as her ongoing struggle with religion, spirituality, and faith. Her poems are perhaps most easily recognized by their unusual style; she invented punctuation marks, capitalized words at will, and forced pauses in reading with her heavy use of dashes, all without regard to the standard rules of grammar, as seen in the following poem:

A Little East of Jordan

A little East of Jordan,
Evangelists record,
A Gymnast and an Angel
Did wrestle long and hard—

Till morning touching mountain—
And Jacob, waxing strong,
The Angel begged permission
To Breakfast—to return!

Not so, said cunning Jacob!
"I will not let thee go
Except thou bless me"—Stranger!
The which acceded to—

Light swung the silver fleeces
"Peniel" Hills beyond,
And the bewildered Gymnast
Found he had worsted God!

Emily was born in 1830 in Amherst, MA, the locale of Amherst College. Her family was intimately involved in the college; her grandfather was one of the founders, her politician father was on the board, and an annual commencement party was held at her home from 1855 onward. The Dickinson family held higher education in very high regard, evidenced by sending Emily's brother Austin to Harvard Law School and Emily herself to Mount Holyoke Female Seminary. Austin successfully completed his formal education and became a respected lawyer in Amherst, but Emily returned home after less than one complete year at Mount Holyoke. Although she was a bright student and charismatic writer, she was not comfortable publicly affirming her faith in Christianity. She was the only student to disobey this order, a decision she later regretted. She was instantly made to feel like an outsider, and when homesickness struck, she set off for Amherst.

Emily spent the rest of her days in increasing isolation from the world outside of Amherst. After her father bought the home in which Emily had spent the first 10 years of her life, called the Homestead, she passed most of her days there with her sister Lavinia and their mother. In 1855 she visited Washington, DC, with Lavinia, and in 1864 and 1865 she saw an eye doctor in Boston. However, upon learning that she suffered an eye condition that was worsened by reading and writing (which the doctor recommended she avoid), she returned to the Homestead permanently. Before this, she would sometimes venture out into the town, but by this time, Emily's brother had married her best friend Susan and they lived in an adjacent property called the Evergreens. Lavinia remained at the Homestead permanently as well, so Emily had no reason to leave.

Emily has been called a recluse, sheltered away from the world, but this is not entirely accurate. She had several very intimate friends with whom she exchanged letters in such quantities that a small fraction of them have been collected into a published book. These friends included Thomas Wentworth Higginson, editor of the *Atlantic Monthly*; Samuel Bowles, editor of the Springfield *Republican*; Helen Hunt Jackson, writer and activist;

and the Reverend Charles Wadsworth. Emily was a prolific writer and sometimes included poems in her letters to friends, but she only published a few poems during her lifetime. All of these were published anonymously—whether she was modest or afraid of criticism is unknown. However, after her death, Lavinia found hundreds of poems stashed in Emily's bedroom. It is estimated that she wrote almost 2,000 poems in her lifetime, many in the late 1850s and early 1860s. Her family and friends published as many as they could in the years following her death, but because of her distinctive style and form, they made many changes to standardize her writing. In later years, efforts were made to reprint her poems more accurately, and most recently, a manuscript was published that includes photocopied originals in the order in which she bound them. Scholars and readers can thus draw their own conclusions about theme and intended meaning from the author's organization rather than the chronological layout in which they were first published.

Emily Dickinson died at the Homestead in 1886 after years of suffering from Bright's disease, a painful kidney disorder. She is buried in Amherst under the epitaph "Called Back."

Theme/Concept

C3

What life theme would you assign to Emily? How did she see her life?

Inference

C2

What evidence from her biography supports your ideas?

Literary Elements

C1

What personal qualities exemplify Emily Dickinson?

EMILY DICKINSON

Creative Synthesis

D3

Create a poem of your own, using Emily's style, to discuss your ideas about the meaning of life.

Summarizing

D2

Summarize Emily's life in a paragraph.

Paraphrasing

D1

In your own words, what do you think Emily Dickinson's epitaph "Called Back" might mean?

EMILY DICKINSON

Reflecting

F3

You may want to live a life quite different from Emily's. What do you see as the advantages and disadvantages of her reclusiveness? Of her coming from an educated family?

Monitoring and Assessing

F2

How will you assess your successes and failures in life? What criteria will you use?

Planning and Goal Setting

F1

Some people would have judged Emily Dickinson to have lived a failed life—she never graduated from college, never married, never left her home. What are your views on her choices in life? How will you plan your life choices 5, 10, 15, and 20 years from now?

EMILY DICKINSON

Harriet Tubman
Social Reformer

Harriet Tubman was born Araminta Ross to slaves Harriet and Ben Ross in Maryland sometime around 1820. No reliable records were kept of slave births, so she may actually have been born as late as 1825. Her owner, Edward Brodess, ran a farm and raised slaves to sell or rent out to nearby plantations for labor. Araminta was first put to work when she was only 6 or 7 years old, taking care of an infant in a home where she was beaten when the baby cried. She was permanently scarred from whippings she received in her childhood, but she was rebellious and clever even at a young age. She began wearing several layers of clothing to protect herself from the whip, but she would cry out as though she was still in excruciating pain so that her masters wouldn't catch on.

In her early teens, Araminta began working in the fields. It was around this time that she began calling herself Harriet, after her mother. One day, while running an errand for her master, she saw a slave attempting to run away. The overseer ordered Harriet to restrain the slave, but she refused, blocking the doorway so the slave could run away. The outraged overseer hurled a 2-pound lead weight that struck Harriet in the head. She was knocked unconscious and remained in a coma for some time. It took her several months to recover, and as soon as she could stand, she was sent back out for hard labor. She sustained permanent damage from this blow and for the rest of her life she suffered from seizures, headaches, and sudden bouts of unconsciousness.

Sometime around 1844, Harriet married a free Black man named John Tubman. However, she was still a slave, so even though she slept at John's house every night, she still had to get up every day and suffer the indignities of slavery. She spoke to her husband about escaping to freedom, but he did not share her rebellious views. He warned her that if she ever tried to escape, he would turn her over to her master. When Brodess died in 1849, though, Harriet's family was at risk of being torn apart forever in separate sales to various landowners. Harriet had heard rumors about the Underground Railroad, a secret connection between homes, or "stations,"

of White and Black abolitionists on the way to Canada and free states in the North. She decided that this was her chance to escape. A White woman who lived nearby gave her a name and directions to the first station she would stop at, and Harriet and two of her brothers ran away on foot in the middle of the night. Her brothers were afraid of the consequences should they be caught, so they turned back. Harriet went on alone, traveling at night, using the North Star as her guide along with help from the Underground Railroad "conductors" she encountered on her path to freedom.

She made it to Philadelphia, PA, and began cooking, cleaning, and saving up to go back and rescue her family. In Philadelphia, she met other abolitionists and determined that her life's calling was to conduct as many slaves to freedom as she possibly could. In 1850, she returned to Maryland and escorted her sister to freedom in Canada. Over the next 7 years, Harriet returned three times to rescue her brothers and parents, relocating all of them to her base of operations in Canada. She tried to bring her husband along with her, but in the time she had been gone, he found another wife. Tubman did not seem to be very affected by this. She continued making trips—19 in all—before the Civil War began. During this time, she acquired several nicknames: "Moses" because she led around 300 people out of slavery and "General Tubman" because of her no-nonsense attitude. Harriet was very serious about getting every one of her "passengers" to safety. To this end, she carried a gun and threatened to shoot anyone who got scared and turned back. She proudly told Frederick Douglass that she "never lost a single passenger," in spite of her uncontrollable sleeping spells. By the time the Civil War began, the reward for Harriet Tubman's capture was $40,000, which today would be equivalent to more than one million dollars. She was well known in the North and the South but still managed to evade capture with help from some famous abolitionist friends, including New York Senator and Abraham Lincoln's future Secretary of State William H.

Seward and his wife. In fact, she stayed in the Sewards' house for a period of time, and in 1859 they sold it to her for a very low price. She moved her family from Canada into the house in Auburn, NY.

Controversial abolitionist John Brown also became a friend to Harriet, and she reportedly helped him plan the raid on Harper's Ferry, VA, in 1859. When the Civil War broke out in 1860, she worked for the Union Army in a variety of ways. She was a cook, nurse, and even a spy, scouting Confederate territories and reporting back to the Union army. In fact, she even commanded a military raid—the first woman to do so—when she led Colonel Montgomery and the men of the 2nd South Carolina regiment in the decimation of Confederate supply depots and freeing of more than 700 slaves. Despite her dedication and service, Tubman was not awarded veteran's pension and therefore struggled financially for the rest of her life.

After the war, she went back to Auburn, NY, and continued her humanitarian work. She took up the suffragist cause, fighting for women's right to vote, and transformed her home into a Home for Aged and Indigent Colored People in 1868. In 1867, John Tubman, no longer connected to Harriet, died. Two years later, Harriet married Nelson Davis, a fellow veteran of the Civil War. That same year, she and Sarah Bradford cowrote her biography, which somewhat eased her money troubles. When her second husband died in 1888, she finally received money from the government in the form of a widow's pension. She was invited to speak publicly and worked closely with the African Methodist Episcopal Zion Church, which would take over running the home she founded when Harriet herself was admitted in 1911. After her death in 1913, she was laid to rest in Fort Hill Cemetery with full military honors.

Consequences and Implications

A3

What were the consequences of Harriet's friendship with the Sewards?

Cause and Effect

A2

What was the impact of the Civil War on Harriet's life?
What was its impact on other Blacks at the time?

Sequencing

A1

What events in Harriet Tubman's early life shaped her later work as an abolitionist? Create a timeline showing the order of major events in her life as chronicled in the biography.

HARRIET TUBMAN

Using Emotion

E3

Many people experience abuse as a child just as Harriet did. How did she use her early experiences to transform herself in adulthood? What negative experiences have you had in your life that can be used for good in the future? Describe and reflect on how to use these experiences to your advantage.

Expressing Emotion

E2

Write a poem or draw a picture to depict your feelings about Harriet's life.

Understanding Emotion

E1

What emotions might Harriet Tubman have had when she was shepherding slaves into freedom? How did others feel about her? Give examples.

HARRIET TUBMAN

Reflecting

F3

Write an essay that describes your reaction to Harriet's accomplishments. What would cause a woman of no means and limited freedom herself to take up the cause of freeing slaves and ultimately helping older adults in the town of Auburn, NY? How do you explain her life mission?

Monitoring and Assessing

F2

Assess the characteristics Harriet displayed in her work as an abolitionist. Which of these do you identify with and why? How would such characteristics help you in your planning to become a professional in a given field?

Planning and Goal Setting

F1

How did Harriet Tubman decide to become a social reformer? What factors influenced her? What factors have influenced you so far in your thinking about a future career?

HARRIET TUBMAN

Name: _____ Date: _____

Margaret Mead
Anthropologist

One of the most widely read anthropologists and greatest minds of the 20th century, Margaret Mead was the first child born to Edward and Emily Fogg Mead in December 1901. They lived in Philadelphia, PA, and soon grew to be a family of six. Hers was a family that valued education, as her father was a professor of finance at the University of Pennsylvania, her mother was a respected sociologist and ethnologist, and her grandmother was a teacher who provided much of Margaret's schooling at home. Emily Mead liberally encouraged her children to pursue their passions and modeled acceptance of individuality. This would heavily influence Margaret's career later in life.

Margaret was initially interested in the humanities: poetry, theater, writing, and psychology. She spent one year of her undergraduate career at DePauw University but transferred to Barnard College in New York, where she got her degree in sociology in 1923. During her senior year, she took an anthropology course taught by Franz Boas, assisted by Ruth Benedict, and discovered her true passion. Ruth became her best friend and remained so throughout her life. Margaret started studying at Columbia University, where she got her master's degree in anthropology in 1925. After graduating, she traveled to Samoa, a Pacific island, to begin her field research.

Three years later, Mead published her first book: *Coming of Age in Samoa*. Her research focused on adolescence, a tumultuous time in the life of the American teenager. To her surprise, she found that the transition from girl to woman was free of psychological distress in Samoa. It was there that she began to conceive of the ideas that would drive much of her later research on the effects of socialization and cultural surroundings compared to biological influences on personality development.

After returning from Samoa, Margaret took the position of assistant curator at the American Museum of Natural History in New York in 1926. Although her professional relationship with the museum would grow over the next 40 years, she continued her research in the field. She conducted

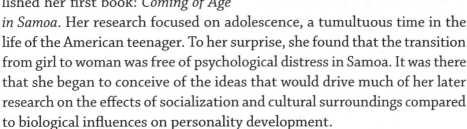

Jacob's Ladder Reading Comprehension Program, Level 5 © Prufrock Press • This page may be photocopied or reproduced with permission for single classroom use. **137**

research with her second husband in New Guinea, studying adolescence in the Manus culture. She published *Growing Up in New Guinea* in 1930 and went right back into the field, studying three different cultures on mainland New Guinea. It was here that she discovered three vastly different sets of gender roles within a small geographical range. *Sex and Temperament in Three Primitive Societies* described the differences between the cultures and compared them to Western conventions. In one culture, the men and women were treated equally and shared equally the burdens of sustaining the family and raising the children. In another, the men and women were aggressive, hostile, and often left the children to tend to themselves. Finally, in the Tchambuli culture, she found a society of dominant women alongside men who looked after the home in what Westerners would call the "housewife" role.

All of these experiences led Margaret to believe that parents' and the culture's expectations shape the behavior of children much more so than biology. She disagreed with the notion that qualities of masculinity or femininity were inherent or genetic. She passionately defended her beliefs in several best-selling books and regular magazine columns. Because she was able to communicate clearly to the public at large, Margaret exposed many Americans to anthropology for the first time. She soon became a hotly debated household name. She welcomed criticism and dissent; she was just pleased that average Americans were discussing cultural anthropology. In 1936, she married her third and final husband, Gregory Bateson. He, like her previous two husbands, was also an anthropologist, and together they traveled and studied in Bali. At this time, film was not being widely used as a research tool, and Margaret was one of the first to document her subjects in photographs.

One of Margaret Mead's greatest contributions to the world was her adherence to a holistic approach to all aspects of life. She had a gift for incorporating every field and illuminating the connections between politics, history, anthropology, psychology, education, science, and so on. Above all, she emphasized the benefits of learning about other cultures in order to think more critically about one's own culture. During World War

II, she and Ruth Benedict helped public policymakers address the issues of encountering many different cultures and soon formed the Institute for Intercultural Studies.

Margaret was crushed when Gregory left her in 1950, but she was likely comforted by her daughter, Mary Catherine Bateson. Doctors had told Margaret during her first marriage that she would never conceive, so Mary Catherine was truly a blessing to her. Mary Catherine made her mother proud by becoming a well-regarded anthropologist in her own right. In 1953, Margaret returned to the Manu culture in Samoa, 25 years after she had studied their young girls' adolescence. She understood the importance of longitudinal studies and encouraged anthropologists, historians, politicians, and the general public to consider changes over biological time rather than calendar years. "Biological time" refers to time as generations—about 25 years per generation. She urged people to be patient when waiting for political or cultural changes, warning against high hopes and promises of quick fixes.

Margaret Mead was truly one-of-a-kind. *TIME* magazine called her "Mother of the World," and by the time she passed away, people had begun referring to her as the grandmother of the world. She was a lecturer, professor at several universities, founder of numerous anthropology departments, and president of quite a few anthropological and scientific societies. She lived a life fuller than most people and died in 1978 of cancer. Margaret was posthumously awarded the Presidential Medal of Freedom. She was an inspiration to many for her contributions and words of wisdom, and notably said, "Never doubt that a small group of thoughtful, committed citizens can change the world. Indeed, it is the only thing that ever has."

Generalizations

B3

What generalizations can you make about Margaret's personal life? About her professional career? What evidence from her biography supports the view that she led a happy life?

Classifications

B2

How would you depict the markers on a charm bracelet? What objects would you use and why?

Details

B1

What were the major markers in Margaret Mead's life that helped her succeed?

MARGARET MEAD

Creative Synthesis

D3

Create a metaphor to represent Margaret's life. It may be an object or a concept. Explain why you have chosen your representation.

Summarizing

D2

Summarize Margaret's life in a paragraph, including early life, education, relationships, and accomplishments.

Paraphrasing

D1

In your own words, describe why Margaret Mead is an important 20th-century figure.

MARGARET MEAD

Reflecting

F3

Margaret's life was one of adventure and breaking new ground in a field called anthropology. As you review her biography, what were the elements that contributed to her success professionally? How might you use them to plot out your own career?

Monitoring and Assessing

F2

Assess the role of education in Margaret's life. What was the nature of its impact on her at different stages? How did her personal relationships contribute to her professional life as well?

Planning and Goal Setting

F1

Based on Margaret Mead's life, what advice would you give to someone wanting to become an anthropologist today?

MARGARET MEAD

Culminating Activities for Biographies

The following section has been created to provide additional challenge for gifted learners and their study of the biographies provided of five famous women who have made contributions to different walks of life. These additional questions and activities may be used in discussion, as written work, or in centers during class time.

Part A

Compare and contrast *three* of the biographies you have read on the following issues:

- What was similar across all three women's stories, even though their contributions were different? _____

_____

_____

- What were the major differences other than contributions made?

_____

_____

- What adversities did they face because of gender, poverty, or illness?

_____

_____

- How did circumstances of birth facilitate or impede the three women you have chosen? _____

_____

_____

- What was the role of education in promoting their talent development? _____

_____

_____

- What was the role of teachers in the lives of these women? How important were they to success in each woman's life?_____

_____

_____

Part B

- If you were to plan your career development path based on the life of one of these women, who would you choose and why? Write an essay describing your choice. _____

_____

_____

- Now, use the biography of the woman you choose as a model for your own career planning effort. Identify your current thinking about a career path. _____

_____

_____

- What goals would you set, based on the model life provided?

_____

_____

- What skills would you like to have and need to develop over the next 3 years in order to move you in the right direction for a chosen career? _____

_____

_____

- What personal qualities would you like to develop or improve?

_____

_____

- What resources (e.g., people, materials, experiences) do you think you will need in the next 3 years to help you? _____

_____

_____

- What criteria would you use to monitor your progress? What might be a timeline for yourself? _____

_____

_____

APPENDIX

A

Pre- and Postassessments and Exemplars

Appendix A contains the pre- and postassessment readings and answer forms, as well as a rubric for scoring the assessments. The preassessment should be administered before any work with *Jacob's Ladder* is conducted. After all readings and questions have been answered, the postassessment can be given to track student improvement on the ladder skill sets. Included in this appendix are example answers for both the pre- and postassessments. The answers are taken from student responses given during the piloting of this curriculum.

Pretest: Emily Dickinson Poem

Please read the poem by Emily Dickinson below. Answer the four questions related to the poem.

This is my letter to the world,
That never wrote to me,—
The simple news that Nature told,
With tender majesty.
Her message is committed
To hands I cannot see;
For love of her, sweet countrymen,
Judge tenderly of me!

1. What does the author think about the world? Provide evidence from the poem to defend your answer.

_____

_____

_____

_____

_____

_____

2. What did the author mean when she wrote, "The simple news that Nature told, / With tender Majesty"? Provide evidence from the poem to defend your answer.

_____

_____

_____

_____

_____

_____

3. What do you think this poem is about? Give a reason why you think so.

_____

_____

_____

_____

_____

_____

4. Create a title for this poem. Give a reason why your title is appropriate for this poem.

_____

_____

_____

_____

_____

_____

Posttest: Emily Dickinson Poem

Please read the poem by Emily Dickinson below. Then answer the four questions related to the poem.

> There is no frigate like a book
> To take us lands away,
> Nor any coursers like a page
> Of prancing poetry.
> This traverse may the poorest take
> Without oppress of toll;
> How frugal is the chariot
> That bears a human soul!

1. What does the author think about books? Provide evidence from the poem to defend your answer.

   _____

   _____

   _____

   _____

   _____

   _____

2. A frigate is a small warship. Why does the author compare a book to a frigate? Provide evidence from the poem to defend your answer.

   _____

   _____

   _____

   _____

   _____

   _____

3. What one word best describes what this poem is about? Give a reason why you think so.

_____

_____

_____

_____

_____

4. Create a title for this poem. Give a reason why your title is appropriate for this poem.

_____

_____

_____

_____

_____

Assessment Scoring Rubric

Question	Points				
	0	**1**	**2**	**3**	**4**
1 Implications and Consequences (Ladder A)	Provides no response or response is inappropriate to the task demand	Limited, vague, inaccurate; rewords the prompt or copies from text	Response is accurate and makes sense but does not adequately address all components of the question or provide rationale from text	Response is accurate; answers all parts of the question; provides a rationale that justifies answer	Response is well written, specific, insightful; answers all parts of the question, offers substantial support, and incorporates evidence from the text
2 Inference (Ladder C)	Provides no response or response is inappropriate to the task demand	Limited, vague, inaccurate; rewords the prompt or copies from text	Accurate response but literal interpretation with no support from the text	Interpretive response with limited support from the text	Insightful, interpretive, well-written response with substantial support from the text
3 Theme/ Generalization (Ladders B and C)	Provides no response or response is inappropriate to the task demand	Limited, vague, inaccurate; rewords the prompt or copies from text	Literal description of the story without explaining the theme; no reasons why	Valid, interpretive response with limited reasoning from the text	Insightful, interpretive response with substantial justification or reasoning
4 Creative Synthesis (Ladder D)	Provides no response or response is inappropriate to the task demand	Limited, vague, inaccurate; rewords the prompt or copies from text	Appropriate but literal title with no attempt to support	Interpretive title with limited reasoning or justification	Insightful, interpretive title with extensive justification or reasoning

Example Answers

Pretest: Emily Dickinson Poem

Note. These answers are based on student responses and teacher ratings from field trials conducted by the Center for Gifted Education and The College of William and Mary. The answers have not been changed from the original student responses.

1. **What does the author think about the world? Provide evidence from the poem to defend your answer.**

   1-point responses might include:

   - The author thinks the world can write.

   - The world doesn't like her.

   - She thinks that no one wrote her back.

   2-point responses might include:

   - I think the author feels good about the world and the way it looks.

   - I think the author thinks the world is graceful, beautiful, and majestic.

   - She loves the earth and everything on it.

   3-point responses might include:

   - She thinks the world is majestic because it says: "The simple news that nature told with tender majesty."

   - The author thinks the world is nice. I think this because she called the world (nature) tender (soft).

   4-point responses might include:

   - What the author thinks of the world is that nature sends a message. I know this because it says "The simple news that nature told."

   - The author thinks the world knows what she's like inside because it said in the poem "To hands I cannot see."

   - I think the author thinks the world is a place to be free because the author can express his or her feelings and write a "letter to the world."

2. **What did the author mean when she wrote "The simple news that Nature told, / With tender majesty"? Provide evidence from the poem to defend your answer.**

1-point responses might include:

- The author means that the world is filled with tender majesty.
- Nature told her thank you.
- Nature was happy.

2-point responses might include:

- I think the author meant that nature was trying to tell her something.
- The author meant that nature tells a story softly and gently.
- She means that people should treat the forests with care.

3-point responses might include:

- I think the author meant that nature told the author a kind message, because tender means kind.
- The author meant that nature was answering her letter and sharing news. She meant that nature was beautiful because if something is majestic that usually means it is beautiful.
- I think she meant the world was good because tender majesty makes me think of a "soft world."

4-point responses might include:

- The author meant that Nature's news was weather because "The simple news" is the rain and snow. Weather can be tender, like soft snow.
- I think it means that nature has shared news with the author. Nature can't speak or write therefore nature has never written to the author but given her news in other ways.
- I think "The simple news that Nature told with tender majesty" means nature is sharing sad news. Because the line "her message is committed" makes the news seem important and the line "for love of her sweet countrymen" sounds like the news is sad.

3. **What do you think this poem is about? Give a reason why you think so.**

1-point responses might include:

- I think this poem is about what the author thinks about the world.

- It's about sending a letter to the world.

- Nature, that's what it talks about the most.

2-point responses might include:

- I think this poem is about how much the author loves the world because she is talking about how beautiful the world is.

- It is about the world because it talks about nature.

- I think this poem is about nature and its message.

3-point responses might include:

- I think it is about how nature relies on people.

- I think it is about the freedom to say what you think.

- This poem is about Mother Nature and the story she tells.

4-point responses might include:

- I think this poem is about a girl who wants to know what the world thinks of her because at the end of the poem she says "Judge tenderly of me."

- I think this poem is about a relative who past away because it said "to hands I can not see." The news that nature told is sad news of a death.

- This poem is about telling the world about pollution but no one will listen. "The simple news nature told me" is Mother Nature is being polluted and so the author is telling the world to stop.

4. **Create a title for this poem. Give a reason why your title is appropriate for this poem.**

1-point responses might include:

- World

- Here's a Letter because the poem is a letter.

- To: World From: Me

2-point responses might include:

- I think The World would be a good title because the whole poem talks about the world.

- My Letter to the World would be a good title because the poem is about someone writing a letter to the world.

- The title should be Nature because the whole poem is about nature.

3-point responses might include:

- The Poem of Love, because it is a touching and sweet poem.

- Majestic World is a good title because one of the lines says "The simple news that nature told, with tender majesty." So this line shows that the author thinks the world is majestic.

- Nature's Message would be a good title because the author talks about nature "talking" to her.

4-point responses might include:

- My title is World Peace. I think it's a good title because the author tells about how tender and sweet the world is. The author says "For love of her" showing that people should protect the world.

- I would name this poem The Message that Never Got Sent because it sounds like the author is trying to tell the world a message about nature but no one is listening.

- The World Should Know. I think this would be a good title because the poem is a letter about what the author thinks is important. The author wants to share what she knows about nature.

Example Answers

Posttest: Emily Dickinson Poem

Note. These answers are based on student responses and teacher ratings from field trials conducted by the Center for Gifted Education at The College of William and Mary. The answers have not been changed from the original student responses.

1. **What does the author think about books? Provide evidence from the poem to defend your answer.**

    1-point responses might include:

    - The author thinks there is no frigate like a book. This evidence is in the first sentence first paragraph.

    - She thinks that books are a frigate which might mean warship.

    - The author thinks books are fun and good.

    2-point responses might include:

    - The author thinks books are like nothing else. I think that because the author says books are not like frigates or courses.

    - She thinks highly of books because she said "There is no frigate like a book" which means that she likes books a whole lot.

    - I think the author likes books because she compared a lot of things to them.

    3-point responses might include:

    - She thinks books are just like frigates because they take you lands away.

    - The author loves books. I know this because during the poem she talks about how books can give you stories you can think up in your imagination.

    - The author thinks that books take you to different places and are good because she says "There is no frigate like a book" and "Nor courses like a page."

    4-point responses might include:

    - Emily Dickinson thinks books are a good way of learning and there are many places to borrow them, like a library where you don't have to pay. I know this because she said "This traverse may the poorest take without oppress of toll."

    - I think the author likes books and really gets into them because she said "there is no frigate like a book to take us lands away." Also, I think she believes every page counts and that they can take you dashing through the story or poem because she said "nor any courses like a page of prancing poetry."

- The author thinks that books can take your mind to distant places without ever leaving your home. I think this because of the sentence from the author's poem: "There is no frigate like a book to take us lands away."

2. **A frigate is a small warship. Why does the author compare a book to a frigate? Provide evidence from the poem to defend your answer.**

1-point responses might include:

- Some books have warships in them.

- They are two things you can see.

- She is comparing a frigate to a book. She said that there is no frigate like a book.

2-point responses might include:

- The author is comparing a book to a frigate because she thinks they are the same.

- She compares a frigate to a book because to her a book is a small warship.

- The author compares a book to a warship because she likes books as much as a small warship.

3-point responses might include:

- She compares the two because when she says "To take us lands away," she means that a book is like a warship. A ship is a form of transportation and a book can make your mind think about the place you are reading about.

- I think the author compared a book to a frigate because she said a book goes to far lands and a frigate travels to lands far away.

- The author compares a book to a frigate because they both bear a human's soul.

4-point responses might include:

- The author compares a frigate to a book because a frigate is small so it can deliver soldiers to far away places and a book can take our imaginations to far away places.

- I think she is trying to say that a book can be powerful, even more powerful than a warship. In the poem she says "There is no frigate like a book to take us lands away, Nor any course like a page."

- She compares a book to a frigate because you can travel to say, Antarctica, just by opening a book. A frigate can also take you to different countries, but it might take hours.

3. **What one word best describes what this poem is about? Give a reason why you think so.**

   1-point responses might include:

   - Frigate
   - Like
   - Neat, because it talks about warships and she uses big and new words.

   2-point responses might include:

   - Books, because she pretty much talks just about books in her story.
   - War! This one word describes the poem because the poem said there is "no frigate like a book."
   - The word I pick is amazing because it is so powerful.

   3-point responses might include:

   - Books, because the author explains why she loves books so much and tells what happens when she reads different kinds of book. She tells what happens in her imagination.
   - Joy would be the one word that best describes what this poem is about. I chose that word because the poem says that books and poetry are really good.
   - Read, I think that because she promotes reading throughout the entire poem.

   4-point responses might include:

   - The one word that best describes what the poem is about is imaginative. I think this because she thinks books take you to mystic places.
   - Relaxing, I chose relaxing because when you read this poem it makes you want to grab a book and get comfortable.
   - Magic, I think that the poem is about the magic of reading. I think that because it talks about where a book can take you.

4. **Create a title for this poem. Give a reason why your title is appropriate for this poem.**

   1-point responses might include:

   - A book.
   - Books and Warships
   - A Poem about Books

2-point responses might include:

- I think a good title for this story might be War because it talks about warships.

- A book because it talks about books.

- Frigate. This is a good name for it because he talks about a frigate.

3-point responses might include:

- I think a good title for this poem is Books because it compares books to other things.

- Read to Find is the title I would pick. I think this because you find out things when you read.

- Read a Book. This title says a lot about the poem, because the author encourages you to read in this poem.

4-point responses might include:

- The Magic of Words. I think it is good because the poem talks about books being magical, taking you to magical places.

- I think The Joy of Reading would be a good title because she talks about enjoying reading in this poem.

- A good title would be All Around the World with a Book. I think this because the poem talks about the many places around the world you can go by reading.

Student Product Task Demand
(Postassessment Only)

Ask students to create an original written piece (it may be a story, a fable, or a poem) that expresses a specific theme of their choosing (e.g., loyalty, redemption, courage). They may use any of the readings in *Jacob's Ladder* as a model for their work. The original piece must tell a story using a main character, a conflict, and a resolution. The selection should focus on providing an engaging plot with appropriate use of structure, detail, images, and symbols. The selection should not exceed 1,000 words. The student should spend one hour planning the piece (e.g., outlining, doing prewriting, doodling, illustrating), 2 hours drafting the piece, one hour proofing and revising, and one hour answering the questions posed below.

Once the piece has been written, proofread, and edited by the student, the following questions should be answered on another piece of paper:

My piece is a _____ (identify genre here) and was modeled after _____ (identify author and title of selection here).

1. What concept did I try to manipulate in my written piece? Why did I choose this concept?

2. What were the story elements that I included (e.g., character, plot, setting, theme)? How did I plan for them? In what order?

3. What images and symbols were used? Why are they significant?

4. What features make my plot engaging?

5. How did I assess my piece critically? What criteria did I apply to judge its effectiveness?

6. As I use the attached rubric to judge my piece, what areas for improvement might I apply to new work? What aspects of the piece did I execute well?

Rubric for Creative Writing

The following items should be assessed, using a 1–4 scale, with 1 being highly ineffective, 2 being ineffective, 3 being effective, and 4 being highly effective. Any item may also receive an N/A, meaning that the criterion was not addressed.

Criteria	Highly Ineffective	Ineffective	Effective	Highly Effective	N/A
The student has organized the piece according to the creative writing model provided.	1	2	3	4	N/A
The student has modeled the elements of a given writing genre in the piece (e.g., poetry, short story, fable).	1	2	3	4	N/A
The student has used an appropriate concept in a complex way.	1	2	3	4	N/A
The student has demonstrated an understanding of how to engage the reader into the plot without making the concept obvious.	1	2	3	4	N/A
The student applies appropriate metacognitive skills to critique work.	1	2	3	4	N/A
The student has included symbols, images, metaphors, or similes to illustrate ideas.	1	2	3	4	N/A

Rubric for Creative Writing, *continued*

What are the major strengths of the written selection?

What are the areas for improvement?

What further readings might enhance student understanding of the creative writing process?

What evidence is provided that the student can use a major concept and story elements to express ideas effectively?

What evidence is provided that the student has developed metacognitive skills of planning, writing, and reflecting?

APPENDIX

B

Record-Keeping Forms/ Documents

Appendix B contains three record-keeping forms and documents:

1. *Brainstorming/Answer Sheet*: This should be given to students for completion after reading a selection so that they may jot down ideas about the selection and questions prior to the discussion. The purpose of this sheet is to capture students' thoughts and ideas generated by reading the text. This sheet should act as a guide when students participate in group or class discussion.

2. *My Reflection on Today's Reading and Discussion*: This form may be completed by the student after a group or class discussion on the readings. The reflection page is designed as a metacognitive approach to help students reflect on their strengths and weaknesses and to promote process skills. After discussion, students use the reflection page to record new ideas that were generated by others' comments and ideas.

3. *Classroom Diagnostic Form*: These forms are for teachers and are designed to aid them in keeping track of the progress and skill mastery of their students. With these charts, teachers can look at student progress in relation to each ladder skill within a genre and select additional ladders and story selections based on student needs.

Name: _____ Date: _____

Brainstorming/Answer Sheet

Use this form to brainstorm thoughts and ideas about the readings and ladder questions before discussing with a partner.

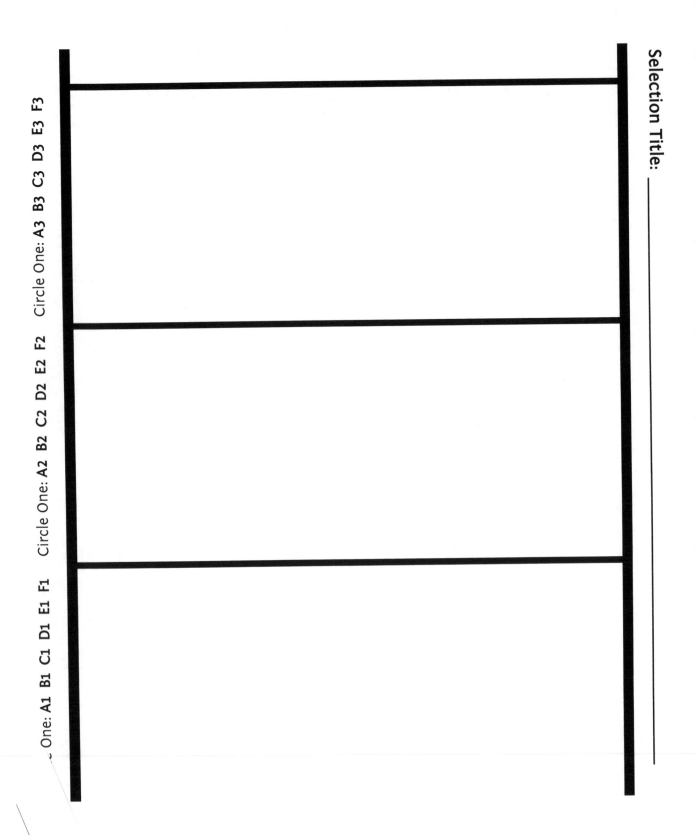

Circle One: A3 B3 C3 D3 E3 F3

Circle One: A2 B2 C2 D2 E2 F2

One: A1 B1 C1 D1 E1 F1

Selection Title: _____

Name: _____ Date: _____

My Reflection on
Today's Reading and Discussion

Selection Title: _____

What I did well:

_____

_____

_____

_____

What I learned:

_____

_____

_____

_____

New ideas I have after discussion:

_____

_____

_____

_____

Next time I need to:

_____

_____

_____

_____

Classroom Diagnostic Form

Short Stories

Use this document to record student completion of ladder sets with the assessment of work.

0 = Needs Improvement   1 = Satisfactory   2 = Exceeds Expectations

Student Name	Mercury and the Sculptor			The Stag at the Pool				The Rocking-Horse Winner			The Gift of the Magi			The Nightingale and the Rose			The Tell-Tale Heart			Ugly			A Haunted House		
	C	D	E	A	B	C	F	A	C	D	C	D	E	A	C	E	C	D	E	B	D	E	A	C	D

Classroom Diagnostic Form
Poetry

Use this document to record student completion of ladder sets with the assessment of work.

0 = Needs Improvement   1 = Satisfactory   2 = Exceeds Expectations

Student Name	Ozymandias				The World Is Too Much With Us				Ulysses					The Lake Isle of Innisfree				In a Library					Fire and Ice				We Wear the Mask		
	A	C	D		C	D	E		C	D	E			C	D	E		A	D	E		A	B	C		A	B	D

Classroom Diagnostic Form

Biographies

Use this document to record student completion of ladder sets with the assessment of work.

0 = Needs Improvement   1 = Satisfactory   2 = Exceeds Expectations

Student Name	Ada Lovelace			Marie Curie			Emily Dickinson			Harriet Tubman			Margaret Mead		
	A	B	C	A	C	F	C	D	F	A	E	F	B	D	F

APPENDIX
C

Alignment to Standards

Appendix C provides teachers with a guide to the content and themes within the readings. For each selection, a chart delineates the national standards addressed by the readings.

Standards Alignment
Short Stories

Language Arts: Short Stories	Mercury and the Sculptor	The Stag at the Pool	The Rocking-Horse Winner	The Gift of the Magi	The Nightingale and the Rose	The Tell-Tale Heart	Ugly	A Haunted House
The student will use analysis of text, including the interaction of the text with reader's feelings and attitudes to create response.	X	X	X	X	X	X	X	X
The student will interpret and analyze the meaning of literary works from diverse cultures and authors by applying different critical lenses and analytic techniques.	X	X		X	X	X		
The student will use knowledge of the purposes, structures, and elements of writing to analyze and interpret various types of text.	X	X	X	X	X	X	X	X
The student will use word-analysis skills, context clues, and other strategies to read fiction and nonfiction with fluency and accuracy.	X	X	X	X	X	X	X	X

Standards Alignment

Poetry

Language Arts: Poetry	Ozymandias	The World Is Too Much With Us, Late and Soon	Ulysses	The Lake Isle of Innisfree	In a Library	Fire and Ice	We Wear the Mask
The student will use analysis of text, including the interaction of the text with reader's feelings and attitudes, to create response.	X	X	X	X	X	X	X
The student will interpret and analyze the meaning of literary works from diverse cultures and authors by applying different critical lenses and analytic techniques.	X		X	X			
The student will use knowledge of the purposes, structures, and elements of writing to analyze and interpret various types of text.	X	X	X	X	X	X	X
The student will use word-analysis skills, context clues, and other strategies to read fiction and nonfiction with fluency and accuracy.	X	X	X	X	X	X	X

Standards Alignment

Biographies

Social Studies and Science Standards	Ada Lovelace	Marie Curie	Emily Dickinson	Harriet Tubman	Margaret Mead
Social Studies Standards					
Culture		X		X	X
People, Places, and Environments	X	X	X	X	X
Individual Development	X	X	X	X	X
Individuals, Groups, and Institutions	X	X	X	X	X
Science Standards					
Science in Personal and Social Perspectives		X			
History and Nature of Science		X			

171

About the Authors

Joyce VanTassel-Baska is the Jody and Layton Smith Professor Emerita of Education and former Executive Director of the Center for Gifted Education at The College of William and Mary in Virginia, where she developed a graduate program and a research and development center in gifted education. She also initiated and directed the Center for Talent Development at Northwestern University. Prior to her work in higher education, Dr. VanTassel-Baska served as the state director of gifted programs for Illinois, as a regional director of a gifted service center in the Chicago area, as coordinator of gifted programs for the Toledo, OH, public school system, and as a teacher of gifted high school students in English and Latin. She is past president of The Association for the Gifted of the Council for Exceptional Children, the Northwestern University Chapter of Phi Delta Kappa, and the National Association for Gifted Children.

Dr. VanTassel-Baska has published widely, including 27 books and more than 500 refereed journal articles, book chapters, and scholarly reports. Recent books include: *Content-Based Curriculum for Gifted Learners* (2011, with Catherine Little), *Patterns and Profiles of Low-Income Learners* (2010), and *Social and Emotional Curriculum With Gifted and Talented Students* (2009, with Tracy Cross and Rick Olenchak). She also served as the editor of *Gifted and Talented International*, a publication of the World Council on Gifted and Talented, for 7 years from 1998–2005.

Tamra Stambaugh is a research assistant professor of special education and director of Programs for Talented Youth at Vanderbilt University. She is the coauthor of *Comprehensive Curriculum for Gifted Learners* and co-editor of *Overlooked Gems: A National Perspective on Low-Income Promising Students*, the *Jacob's Ladder Reading Comprehension Program* (both with Joyce VanTassel-Baska) and *Leading Change in Gifted Education* (with Bronwyn MacFarlane). Stambaugh has also authored or coauthored journal articles and book chapters on a variety of topics focusing on curriculum, instruction, and leadership. Her current research interests include the impact of accelerated curriculum on student achievement, teacher effectiveness, and talent development factors—especially for students of poverty.

Dr. Stambaugh serves as a member of the National Association for Gifted Children's professional standards committee and the Higher Education workgroup. She is the recipient of several awards, including the Margaret The Lady Thatcher Medallion for scholarship, service, and character from The College of William and Mary School of Education. Prior to her appointment at Vanderbilt, she was director of grants and special projects at The College of William and Mary, Center for Gifted Education, where she also received her Ph.D. in educational planning, policy, and leadership with an emphasis in gifted education and supervision.